SPREADSHEETS
&
DATABASES

Training material

CAMILLA BRADLEY

JOHN MURRAY

By the same author:

Introducing Word Processing

Continuing Word Processing

© Camilla Bradley 1992

First published 1992 by
John Murray Publishers Ltd
50 Albemarle Street
London W1X 4BD

Designed and typeset by Gecko Ltd, Bicester, Oxon

Printed in Great Britain by St Edmundbury Press Ltd,
Bury St Edmunds

Bound by Hunter & Foulis, Edinburgh

A catalogue entry for this title is available from the British Library

ISBN 0-7195-5072-6

Contents

Introduction

Who the book is for

This book consists of carefully graded tasks which are designed to give 'hands-on' experience in the use of spreadsheets and databases. It is designed for several groups of users.

(1) The student studying for the RSA Certificate in Computer Literacy and Information Technology or similar qualification will find it builds up the skills required for tackling the end-of-course assignments.

(2) NVQ Level I and II Business Administration students can use it to gain a good grounding in the practical competencies required by the module specifications.

(3) The 16-plus age group in Years 12 and 13 at school studying Information Technology will find it provides them with the basic skills required to manipulate the software packages.

(4) Open Learning and workshop-based students can work their way through the book with minimal tutor support, provided they have been given the software keystroke instructions.

How the book is organised

The book analyses the essential components of spreadsheet and database software packages. Each unit starts with an explanation and pictorial description of the unit's objectives, which the user will be expected to attain in the following tasks.

The tasks have been carefully graded to build up skills, and they follow a sequence. They must be performed in order, if all the components of the software are to be covered. Their aim is to prepare the student for assessed coursework, and they give sufficient practice in the basic software skills to enable students to cope with this.

The book is aimed directly at the student. The text is supported with illustrated examples, and the functions used to tackle each batch of tasks have been specified. The content of the tasks is of a very general nature, spanning a wide range of subjects, including some from the commercial world.

Though it is necessary for the tutor to provide instructions on the keystrokes used to operate the software, the student should be able to work his or her way through the tasks unaided. As the tasks are all to be printed out, the student will end up with a 'folder of work', should this be required as part of the assessment procedures. The tasks are, therefore, addressed to the student, and give practice in following simple instructions as well as in manipulating the software.

What is a spreadsheet?

A spreadsheet is a computer program which is used to do calculations and accounting. It takes away the chore of entering headings and numbers by hand on paper and using a calculator to work out the totals. Alterations and recalculations can be done with a few keystrokes, so a spreadsheet is a quick and powerful program for anyone using numerical data.

A spreadsheet always has a tabular form although it is not ruled up like ledger paper. The screen is marked like a grid with lettered columns running across the top, and numbered rows running down the left-hand side.

The **columns** are labelled with the letters of the alphabet from A to Z, but if the spreadsheet is very wide, they continue with AA, AB, AC, ..., AZ and then BA, BB, BC, ..., BZ and so on. The **rows** are numbered, starting with row 1 and continuing to whatever maximum the particular spreadsheet program will allow.

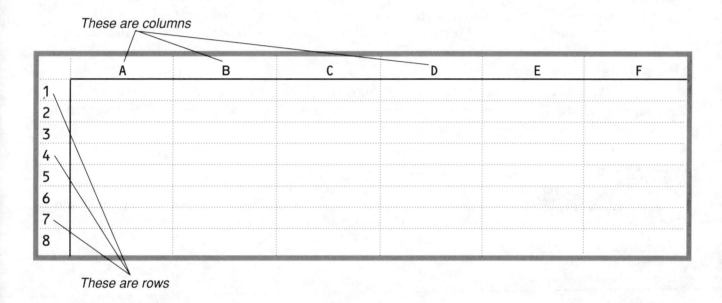

These are columns

These are rows

The position on the screen where a column and a row intersect is called a **cell**. Each cell is referred to by its column and row number; for example, A1, A6, B3, D5 – to name a few cells at random. On the screen, the current cell is highlighted by a **cursor** or **cell pointer**. Only one cell can be high-lighted at a time, and it is always the cell in which work is being carried out.

The cursor is in cell D7

	A	B	C	D	E	F
1	SALES OF STATIONERY PRODUCTS					
2						
3		JANUARY	FEBRUARY	MARCH		
4	Pencils	90	87	59		
5	Rulers	43	36	20		
6	Blue biros	85	73	68		
7	Black biros	101	120			
8	Rubbers					
9						
10	TOTAL SALES					

■ *Typical features of a spreadsheet*

All spreadsheets have certain features in common although each one has its own particular operating instructions.

Entering data

Text and numbers can be entered for descriptive purposes, that is, to provide headings. The usual term for this is **labels**. Numbers can also be entered as a basis for a calculation. These numbers are known as **values**.

Performing calculations

A calculation can only be performed by writing a **formula**, that is, a set of special instructions. The formulae can be very simple or very complex, depending on the calculation required. Common calculations use simplified formulae called **functions**.

Copying information

Once information has been entered on a spreadsheet, it can be copied (or **replicated**) anywhere else, if need be. Labels, values and formulae can all be copied and do not have to be entered again.

Alterations

These can take the form of recalculating the contents, or revising the layout. Recalculations are done automatically. If one number is changed, any others that are affected are changed too. Corrections can also easily be made to the layout.

Forecasting

Spreadsheets are a powerful tool for financial forecasting. They can be used to construct 'What if …' tables which project a new value into a calculation. For example, a 'What if …' table could be used to show how monthly repayments on a loan would differ if the rate of interest altered.

A typical spreadsheet would look something like this:

Labels (or text)   Values (figures for calculation)

	A	B	C	D	E	F
1	BRADLEY'S SANDWICH BAR EXPENSES TO 31 MARCH					
2						
3		January	February	March		
4	EXPENSES					
5	Rent	1,000.00	1,000.00	1,000.00		
6	Utilities	900.00	1,200.00	800.00		
7	Advertising	500.00	300.00	400.00		
8	Salaries	1,500.00	1,500.00	1,500.00		
9	Goods sold	4,000.00	3,800.00	4,500.00		
10						
11	TOTAL	7,900.00	7,800.00	8,200.00		

C11 TOTAL C5:C9

Cursor in cell C11

Formula for calculating the total of column C from cell C5 to cell C9

Setting up a spreadsheet

In Unit 1, you will learn to prepare the layout of your spreadsheet, but you will not perform any calculations. You will learn how to complete four essential functions apart from printing. These are:

- Entering labels and values

- Widening the columns

- Changing the numeric display format

- Changing the position of labels

Labels and values

A **label** is the name given to a piece of text, but it also refers to numbers which are there for descriptive purposes, and do not form part of a calculation. Dates are labels because they do not form part of a calculation. Labels may have to be entered on a spreadsheet in a special way.

	A	B	C	D	E	F
1	October 1991 Bookings					
2						
3		Tour 147	Tour 292	Tour 865		
4	8/10/91					
5	15/10/91					
6	22/10/91					

Examples of different kinds of labels

A **value** is the name given to a number which will be used later as part of a calculation. For example, numbers in a column which are going to be added up are all values. There may be different rules for entering values on a spreadsheet from entering labels, and you must make sure you know what they are.

	A	B	C	D	E	F
1	October 1991 Bookings					
2						
3		Tour 147	Tour 292	Tour 865		
4	8/10/91	2,400	1,733	1,059		
5	15/10/91	579	284	360		
6	22/10/91	153	97	101		

The same spreadsheet which now contains values

Before you start on the tasks, you should write down in a notebook the keystrokes you use, as you will need this information for reference purposes.

Function	Keystrokes used
Enter labels	....
Enter values	....
Correct keying in errors	....
Delete an incorrect entry	....
Print the spreadsheet	....

Task 1

Load the spreadsheet program so that the column and row display is on screen, and the cursor is in cell A1. Enter headings across the top of the spreadsheet as shown, then enter the text in the first two columns. To do this, you may have to use the special instructions for entering *labels*. Then enter numbers in the third column. To do this, you may have to use the special instructions for entering *values*.

```
TASK 1

FRUIT          ORIGIN      LBS SOLD

APPLE          ENGLAND         132
APRICOT        FRANCE            8
BANANA         JAMAICA         165
GRAPE          ITALY            75
MANGO          KENYA             8
MELON          CYPRUS          104
NECTARINE      FRANCE           49
ORANGE         ISRAEL          115
PEACH          SPAIN            23
PINEAPPLE      KENYA            37
```

When you have completed the entries on your spreadsheet, check that they are correct, then print it.

Load the spreadsheet program so that the column and row display is on screen and the cursor is in cell A1. Enter headings across the top of the spreadsheet as shown, then enter the text in the first two columns. If you have to use different instructions for labels and values, you may find it easier to enter the labels (text) first, and then to enter the values (numbers).

```
TASK 2

NAME              RESULT          MARK

Adams  P          Pass            50
Brown  B          Pass            55
Evans  M          Credit          70
Harrison  T       Referred        46
Lynch  T          Fail             8
Manning  A        Credit          68
Shah  R           Pass            56
Stephens  M       Pass            52
Thompson  N       Fail             9
Wilson  C         Pass            57
```

When you have completed the entries on your spreadsheet, check that they are correct, then print it.

■ *Widening the columns*

Spreadsheet columns have a set width, which is usually ten spaces. This means that if you key in a label that is longer than the width of the column, the label may be cut short.

This is certain to happen if there is an entry in the cells to the right of the long label. If there is no entry in the cells to the right of the long label – for example, if it is a spreadsheet heading – it will probably extend into the adjoining columns.

Label extending into adjoining columns

	A	B	C	D	E	F
1	FIGURES FOR FRESH FRUIT IMPORTS					
2						
3		Jan	Feb	March	April	
4	Bananas	300	390	450	552	
5	Oranges	980	752	466	748	
6	Grapes	753	894	550	649	
7	Strawberri	109	588	743	920	

Label cut short because of entry in adjoining cell

Values may also be cut short if they are too long to fit the normal column width. Your spreadsheet may give you a warning signal if this likely to be the case, as terrible errors can result if numeric entries are cut short.

It is possible to adjust the width of columns in a spreadsheet. They can be made wider so that a long label is displayed completely even when there are entries in the adjoining cells.

In the example given, the first column must be at least twelve spaces wide in order to display the word **Strawberries** completely. However, it would be wise to make it 13 spaces wide to allow a gap before the start of the next column.

	A	B	C	D	E	F
1	FIGURES FOR FRESH FRUIT IMPORTS					
2						
3		Jan	Feb	March	April	
4	Bananas	300	390	450	552	
5	Oranges	980	752	466	748	
6	Grapes	753	894	550	649	
7	Strawberries	109	588	743	920	

Column A has been widened to allow a long label to be displayed

In the next two tasks, you will practise widening columns on the spreadsheet to deal with longer entries.

Before you start on the tasks, you should write down in a notebook the keystrokes you use, as you will need this information for reference purposes.

Function	Keystrokes used
Widen a column	....

Task 3

Make sure you know how many characters you can normally fit into a column with the spreadsheet program you are using. Probably, it will be ten characters, but this may not be the case.

Then look down the first column, and count the characters in the longest word. This is the width you will have to make column A. It is advisable to increase this number by one, so there is a space between column A and column B, both on the screen and when you print out.

Next, count up the characters (and spaces, if any) in the longest entry in column B. If necessary, increase this number by one. Then, widen column A and column B. When this is done, enter the column headings, the labels and values.

When you have completed the task, print it out.

```
TASK 3

DISTANCES FROM LONDON

TOWN                COUNTY               MILES

Wolverhampton       West Midlands          129
Middlesbrough       Cleveland              250
Liverpool           Merseyside             210
Peterborough        Cambridgeshire          82
Corby               Northamptonshire        85
Aylesbury           Buckinghamshire         41
Huddersfield        West Yorkshire         190
Basingstoke         Hampshire               49
Bournemouth         Dorset                 106
Luton               Bedfordshire            32
```

Before you start to enter Task 4, make sure you know how many characters you can normally fit into a column with the spreadsheet program you are using. Probably, it will be ten characters, but this may not be the case.

Then look down the first column in Task 4, and count the characters in the longest word. This is the width you will have to make column A. It is advisable to increase this number by one, so there is a space between column A and column B, both on the screen and when you print out.

Next, do the same for the remaining columns and widen them if necessary before keying in the entries.

When you have completed the task, print it out.

```
TASK 4

INDEPENDENT LOCAL GROCERY CHAINS

AREA                NAME                LOCATION      NO OF STORES

West Yorkshire      Pennine Stores      City centre            16
Humberside          Viking Grocery      City centre             7
Liverpool           City Food Chain     City centre             3
Gt Manchester       Piccadilly Foods    Out of town            12
Nottingham/Derby    Fresh Foods Ltd     Out of town            14
Preston/Blackpool   Red Rose Grocers    Out of town            14
South Yorkshire     Hallam Markets      City centre             5
Teeside             T Supermarkets      Out of town            10
Tyne and Wear       Metro Stores        City centre             6
Wolverhampton       Multistores Ltd     City centre             3
```

Formatting numbers

In Tasks 5 and 6, you are going to practise entering values (numbers) using different styles. This is called **numeric display formatting**.

General format

When this format is used, numbers are not displayed with commas separating the hundreds from the thousands, and trailing zeros after a decimal point may not be shown.

	A	B	C	D	E	F
1	FRESH FISH IMPORTS IN TONS					
2						
3		Jan-June	July-Dec			
4	Cod	45700	59865			
5	Plaice	32550	39600			
6	Haddock	7900	7750			

An example of general format

Punctuated format

In this format a comma is always displayed between the hundreds and thousands, even though it may not actually have been keyed in. For example, **17963** is displayed and printed as **17,963**.

	A	B	C	D	E	F
1	FRESH FISH IMPORTS IN TONS					
2						
3		Jan-June	July-Dec			
4	Cod	45,700	59,865			
5	Plaice	32,550	39,600			
6	Haddock	7,900	7,750			

An example of punctuated format

Fixed decimal format

This means that a fixed number of decimal places are displayed after a decimal point. Sometimes it is referred to as a 'pounds and pence format' if two decimal places only are displayed.

	A	B	C	D	E	F
1	FRESH FISH IMPORTS IN TONS					
2						
3		Jan-June	July-Dec			
4	Cod	45700.00	59865.00			
5	Plaice	32550.00	39600.00			
6	Haddock	7900.00	7750.00			

An example of fixed decimal format

Function	Keystrokes used
Select general format	....
Select punctuated format	....
Select fixed decimal format (i.e. pounds and pence format)	....

Task 5

In Task 5 you must key in a heading, and enter the values (numbers) in the last two columns using the 'pounds and pence' format which displays two decimal places. The last column must also have a 'punctuated format' which displays a comma between the hundreds and the thousands.

Remember that the numbers in the first column can be entered as labels (text), as they are purely descriptive, and would not be used in a calculation.

When the task is complete, print it out.

```
TASK 5

YEARLY CARPET SALES IN £

STOCK NO    DESIGN          PRICE         SALES

6480        Woodland        13.25     58,000.00
6481        Chelsea         27.95     93,500.00
6482        Primavera        9.99      9,699.00
6483        Mandarin        11.50     54,600.00
6484        Rhapsody        10.95      6,333.00
6485        Edwardian       31.00     27,900.00
6486        Festival        24.99     90,000.00
6487        Henley          28.50      5,650.00
6488        Flora            9.99     72,050.00
6489        Dolce Vita      33.00     29,655.00
```

In Task 6 you must enter a heading and widen the columns where necessary. Enter the values (numbers) in column C using a 'pounds and pence' format which displays two decimal places, and enter the values (numbers) in column D using a 'punctuated format' which displays a comma between the hundreds and the thousands.

Remember that the numbers in the first column can be entered as labels (text), as they are purely descriptive, and would not be used in a calculation. It is only in columns C and D that you are entering values.

When the task is complete, print it out.

TASK 6

HALF YEARLY SALES OF SPORTS EQUIPMENT

REF	DESCRIPTION	PRICE	NO SOLD
40	Leather football	6.49	7,450
17	Football gloves	4.99	1,300
93	Badminton racket	7.79	922
82	Squash racket	19.99	430
51	Snooker cue	19.99	2,960
97	Snooker table	59.99	29
23	Set of dumbbells	13.99	740
18	Exercise bike	69.99	37
14	Rowing machine	59.99	9
68	Punchbag	36.99	54

Positioning entries

When values are entered on a spreadsheet, they are always positioned at the right-hand edge of the cell. It is not possible to change their position, only their format – which you have been doing in the previous two tasks.

Labels can have three different positions in a cell, and different instructions must be given for each of the positions a label can have.

(1) They can be entered at the right-hand edge.

(2) They can be entered in the centre.

(3) They can be entered at the left-hand edge.

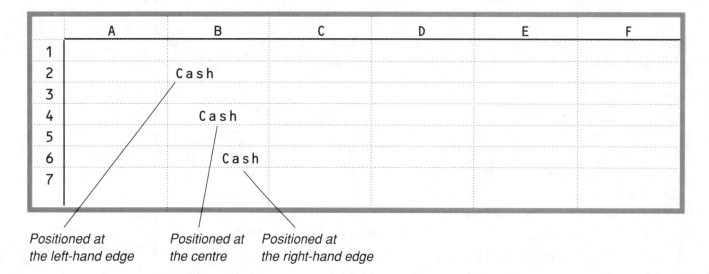

Positioned at the left-hand edge

Positioned at the centre

Positioned at the right-hand edge

Making corrections

If an entry in a cell has to be changed, the existing entry may have to be deleted before a new entry can be made. It may not be possible to replace the entry in a cell without deleting the original entry first. You have already learnt how to make corrections by deleting incorrect entries, but you should check your spreadsheet to see if this method of replacing cell entries is used.

Moving round a spreadsheet

Moving round a spreadsheet cell by cell is very time-consuming. It is usually possible to move straight to a specific cell so that entries or corrections can be made.

Before you start on the next tasks, you should write down in a notebook the keystrokes you use, as you will need this information for reference purposes.

Function	Keystrokes used
Position label at right-hand edge of cell	....
Position label at centre of cell	....
Position label at left-hand edge of cell	....
Replace a cell entry	....
Move to a specific cell	....

Task 7

In Task 7 you are going to concentrate on making corrections to your spreadsheet before you print it out. You will make these corrections by replacing incorrect information in cells.

In addition, you must format the first column so that the entries line up on the right-hand side. This is the normal position for values (numbers), but so far you have always entered labels (text) so that they line up on the left-hand side.

```
TASK 7


OFFICE STATIONERY SALES


                    1ST QTR      2ND QTR      3RD QTR      4TH QTR
       PURCHASES       £            £            £            £
    Headed paper      107          220          136           94
   A4 bond paper       86           74           20           20
   A5 bond paper       23           25           25           30
   Yellow flimsy       12           22           15           35
   Carbon paper        32           38           40            8
 S/hand notepads        4            8           12           16
    Message pads        8           12           16           15
    C6 envelopes      110          200           98           70
```

Before printing out the spreadsheet, make the following corrections.

OFFICE STATIONERY SALES

	1ST QTR	2ND QTR	3RD QTR	4TH QTR
PURCHASES	£	£	£	£
Letter head ~~Headed paper~~	107	220	136	94
A4 bond paper	86	74	~~20~~ 120	~~20~~ 120
A5 bond paper	23	25	25	30
Bank paper ~~Yellow flimsy~~	12	22	15	35
Carbon paper	32	~~38~~ 28	40	8
S/hand notepads	4	8	12	~~16~~ 6
Note ~~Message~~ pads	8	12	16	15
C6 envelopes	110	200	98	70
Add two more rows { Labels	19	14	7	9
Corrector	10	8	12	7

When you have completed the corrections, print out the spreadsheet.

Task 8

In Task 8 you are again going to concentrate on making corrections to your spreadsheet before you print it out. You will make these corrections by replacing incorrect cell entries.

In addition, you must format the columns so that the entries line up on the right-hand side. This is the normal position for values (numbers), but so far you have usually entered labels (text) so that they line up on the left-hand side.

```
TASK 8

CADOGAN CURTAINS - PRICE LIST WITH LENGTH IN INCHES

        STYLE    54" DROP      72" DROP      90" DROP

        Cameo       45.00         49.00         54.00
       Chintz       35.00         40.00         45.00
Country Style       85.00         95.50        105.00
      Garland       40.00         45.00         49.00
   Kingfisher      100.00        110.00        118.00
     Nautical       49.00         55.00         62.00
    Springtime      79.00         85.00         93.00
       Tahiti       39.50         45.00         52.00
```

Before printing your spreadsheet, make some alterations.

(1) Add an extra column on the right entitled **108" DROP**. The entries for this column are **59, 50, 115, 53, 124, 67, 100, 59.**

(2) **Country Style** is now called **Country Life**.

(3) The price for **Nautical 90" DROP** is **61.00.**

(4) The price for **Springtime 72" DROP** is **86.00.**

(5) The price for **Tahiti 54" DROP** is **38.00.**

(6) Add an extra row at the end of the spreadsheet with entries as follows:
Westmoreland 95 105 114 123

(7) Print out your spreadsheet.

Often, a task may be presented in a different way. The spreadsheet may not already be written out ready for you to copy. You may just be given a list of instructions to follow, and the design of the spreadsheet may be left entirely for you to decide upon.

In this task, you will still only be preparing the layout for the spreadsheet, as you have not yet learnt how to perform calculations. This task is presented as a list of instructions for you to follow, instead of a ready-made spreadsheet for you to copy.

(1) Load your spreadsheet program.

(2) Enter the title of the spreadsheet: `DISK PRICES PER BOX`

(3) Starting from the second column, enter the following headings:
`QTY 1-4   QTY 5-9   QTY 10+`

(4) In the first column enter the following titles (left-justified):
`DATAX`
`GLOBAL`
`MICCO`
`OMNIUM`
`STAR`

(5) Enter the data shown below using a numeric format with two decimal places.

	QTY 1-4	QTY 5-9	QTY 10+
DATAX	12.45	11.95	11.45
GLOBAL	11.20	10.60	9.95
MICCO	14.40	13.55	12.95
OMNIA	11.55	10.75	10.20
STAR	11.45	10.30	9.75

(6) Check your spreadsheet carefully, then alter the `OMNIA` prices to `11.50`, `10.70` and `10.15`.

(7) Add an extra entry to the end of the spreadsheet:
`VERITY   11.95   10.95   10.50`

(8) Alter the price for `DATAX QTY 1-4` to `12.50`.

(9) Alter the name `MICCO` to `MICROCO`.

(10) Print out your spreadsheet.

Task 10 – Christmas shopping spreadsheet

For Task 10, set up your own spreadsheet giving details of your ideas for Christmas presents.

Make a list of all the people you would normally give presents to, and what you intend to give each of them this year. The list may look something like this.

```
Grandad
Grandma
Mum
Dad
Sister
Brother
Boyfriend/Girlfriend
Schoolfriend
```

Decide where you are planning to do your shopping, and enter the names of the shops in your spreadsheet. Then enter the maximum price you intend spending on each item, using the 'pounds and pence' format. Print out your spreadsheet.

Your spreadsheet should now have four columns and look something like the one shown below.

```
CHRISTMAS  SHOPPING

PERSON                  GIFT        PRICE        NAME OF SHOP

Grandad
Grandma
Mum
Dad
Sister
Brother
Boyfriend/Girlfriend
Schoolfriend
```

Now practise making alterations. See if you can add some more people, perhaps cousins, to the end of your spreadsheet.

Alter the prices to make your money stretch further. You may want to make some further alterations to your spreadsheet, like changing the gifts you have chosen, or the shops you intend to visit.

When your revised spreadsheet is complete, print it out.

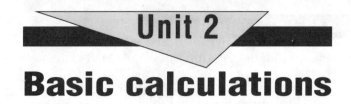
Unit 2

Basic calculations

In Unit 2 you will see how a spreadsheet allows calculations to be performed simply and easily on numerical data by using functions. You will also learn how to define the range of cells in which you want the calculations performed, and to copy (replicate) the function for standard calculations across your spreadsheet. In addition, you will start to save your spreadsheet so that you can retrieve it for later use. This unit will, therefore, concentrate on the following:

■ Using a function

■ Defining ranges

■ Replication

■ Saving and retrieving

■ Using a function

A calculation is performed on a spreadsheet by using a simple instruction. If a standard calculation is to be performed a special ready-made instruction is provided, and this is known as a **function**. Totalling a column of figures or finding the average of a set of data are examples of the sort of standard calculations for which functions are used.

Any function that is used, is displayed on screen and will give the name of the function and the cells which are involved in the calculation.

Below is an example of a function used to give the total of a column of figures.

	A	B	C	D	E	F
1		Jan	Feb	Mar		
2	Clothes	89	25	102		
3	Newspapers	8	7	14		
4	Transport	100	93	97		
5						
6	TOTAL	197	125	213		

D6 TOTAL D2:D4

A function used to total cells D2, D3 and D4

Cursor is in cell D6 where the result of the function appears

When using functions, it is common to specify the cells which are involved in the calculation. The example given above is **D6 TOTAL D2:D4**. This means add the figures in all the cells from cell D2 to cell D4 and display the result in cell D6.

Using a range of cells

When performing calculations a **range** or block of cells is normally involved. The most common ranges are either a column of cells or a row of cells. However, ranges can also consist of several columns or several rows. What the spreadsheet cannot recognise as a range is any L-shaped block of cells.

These are common ranges.

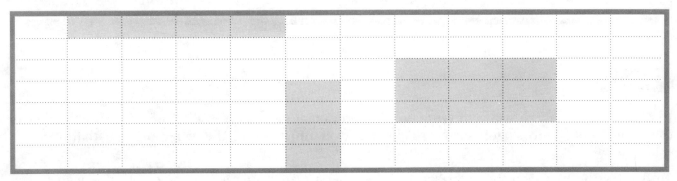

These are not recognised as ranges.

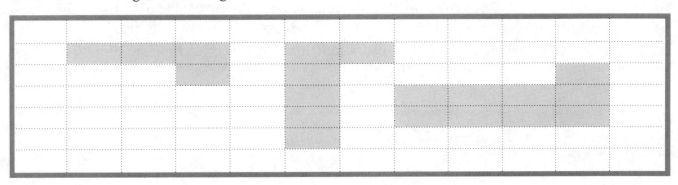

A function normally involves a calculation over a range of cells, so it is necessary to state the range of cells that is involved. The usual way of doing this is to give the first cell and the last cell involved in the calculation.

	A	B	C	D	E	F
1		1st qtr	2nd qtr	3rd qtr	4th qtr	TOTAL
2						
3	Carrots	500	600	550	750	2,400
4	Cauliflower	700	900	1,200	2,400	
5	Green peas	1,300	1,400	1,500	2,000	

In this example, for the total to appear in cell F3, the range involved is B3 to E3.

	A	B	C	D	E	F
1		1st qtr	2nd qtr	3rd qtr	4th qtr	TOTAL
2						
3	Carrots	500	600	550	750	2,400
4	Cauliflower	700	900	1,200	2,400	
5	Green peas	1,300	1,400	1,500	2,000	
6						
7	TOTAL	2,500				

In this example, for the total to appear in cell B7, the range involved is B3 to B5.

Function	Keystrokes used
Using a function to get a total	....
Defining a range	....

Task 11

In Task 11 you will be using the function for producing a total. You will have to total the values (numbers) both across and down. To do this, you must quote the *range* of cells that you are totalling.

To display the totals on the right-hand side of the spreadsheet, the cursor must be placed in the TOTAL column, and the range will include the cells from LONDON to WALES in each row.

To display the totals at the bottom of the spreadsheet, the cursor must be placed in the TOTAL row, and the range will include the cells from Waltz to Folk in each column.

Enter the spreadsheet shown below, then use a function and range to complete the totals. When your spreadsheet is complete, print it out.

```
TASK 11

DANCING COMPETITION

              LONDON      MIDLANDS    THE NORTH    WALES    TOTAL

Waltz         5           3           6            8
Latin         7           9           8            7
Disco         6           7           6            9
Formation     9           8           8            6
Modern        7           6           5            4
Cabaret       5           8           4            5
Folk          4           6           6            8

TOTAL
```

Task 12

In Task 12 you are required to total the sales figures to give the yearly and quarterly demand a newsagent has for a variety of magazines. By doing this, it is possible to see which magazines are more popular than others, and at which times of the year magazines sell best.

Enter the spreadsheet as shown, and then use a function to calculate the yearly sales for each magazine. These will appear in the TOTAL column at the right-hand side of the spreadsheet.

Then use a function to calculate the quarterly sales for the selection of magazines. These will appear in the TOTAL row at the bottom of the spreadsheet.

In this task, you must total the sales one by one, though you will soon learn how to replicate the totals rather than entering them one at a time.

When you have completed all the totals, print out your spreadsheet.

```
TASK 12

YEARLY MAGAZINE SALES


TITLE           1ST QTR    2ND QTR    3RD QTR    4TH QTR    TOTAL


21 Today          540        300        250        490
Chatterbox        560        330        460        600
Chic              250        150        180        220
Heaven Sent        90        150        120         80
Just 16           210        140        170        200
Londoner          330        290        300        350
Music Now          80         75         75         90
Ooh!               85         75         80         80
Smart Set         650        680        680        590
Teenagers          80         75         80         90


TOTAL
```

Function	Keystrokes used
Using a function to get an average	....
Defining a range	....

Task 13

In this task, you will be using the function for finding the **average** of a list of figures. You will have to average the values (numbers) both across and down. To do this, you must quote the *range* of cells that you are totalling.

To display the averages on the right-hand side of the spreadsheet, the cursor must be placed in the AVERAGE column, and the range will include the cells from YR 1 to YR 5.

To display the averages at the bottom of the spreadsheet, the cursor must be placed in the AVERAGE row, and the range will include the cells from Sales to Office services.

Enter the spreadsheet, then use a function and range to complete the averages. When your spreadsheet is complete, print it out.

TASK 13

DAYS LOST THROUGH ILLNESS

DEPARTMENT	YR 1	YR 2	YR 3	YR 4	YR 5	AVERAGE
Sales	46	39	34	30	33	
Personnel	11	6	9	14	17	
Accounts	20	19	19	28	31	
Purchasing	26	25	22	18	27	
Marketing	43	53	51	58	52	
Office services	20	33	17	25	18	
AVERAGE						

In Task 14 you will be required to find out the average calories lost for each type of activity and the total number of calories lost by people of different weights who indulge in all of them.

You must enter the spreadsheet as shown, and then use a function to calculate the average calories for each type of activity. These will appear in the AVERAGE column at the right-hand side of the spreadsheet.

Then, you must use a function to calculate the total calories lost by partaking in all these activities. These will appear in the TOTAL row at the bottom of the spreadsheet.

In this task, you must enter the average and totals one by one, though you will soon learn how to replicate the averages and totals rather than entering them one at a time.

When you have completed the calculations, print out your spreadsheet.

```
TASK 14

CALORIES USED IN 10 MINUTES' ACTIVITY

WEIGHT IN LB:        125        150        175        200        AVERAGE

Cycling              40         50         60         65
Disco dancing        60         65         70         75
Football             80         90         100        110
Housework            35         40         50         55
Jogging              90         110        125        140
Office work          25         30         35         40
Sleeping             10         10         15         15
Swimming             70         90         100        110
Walking              30         35         40         45
Watching TV          10         10         15         15

TOTAL
```

Replication

Instead of entering totals one by one, which is very time-consuming, it is normal to use the **replicate** command to copy your instructions down a column or across a row. This will make it quicker to perform calculations when several columns or rows of figures are involved.

When a function is used for a calculation, the result of the calculation is displayed on screen in the cell where the cursor is placed. For example, in the spreadsheet below, cell D3 displays the result of adding together the contents of cell B3 and cell C3.

Cell D3 displays the result of adding together the figures for areas 1 and 2.

	A	B	C	D	E	F
1	ITEM SOLD	AREA 1	AREA 2	TOTAL		
2						
3	Blouses	4,500	5,000	9,500		
4	Cardigans	1,000	1,300			
5	Dresses	900	950			
6	Jumpers	2,600	2,300			
7	Skirts	700	850			

D3 TOTAL B3:C3

The function used for adding together the figures in cells B3 and C3.

By giving a replicate command, it is possible to copy the function, so that the remaining cells also display the total for areas 1 and 2. Obviously, it is much quicker to do this than to enter the totals one by one.

Cell D3 displays the result of adding together the figures for areas 1 and 2.

	A	B	C	D	E	F
1	ITEM SOLD	AREA 1	AREA 2	TOTAL		
2						
3	Blouses	4,500	5,000	9,500		
4	Cardigans	1,000	1,300	2,300		
5	Dresses	900	950	1,850		
6	Jumpers	2,600	2,300	4,900		
7	Skirts	700	850	1,550		

The function used for adding together the figures for areas 1 and 2 has been copied into the range of cells from D4 to D7.

In these examples, replication has only been used to copy the function which gives the total of a set of figures. It can, of course, be used in all sorts of different calculations, and not just when you want to produce a total.

Function	Keystrokes used
Replicate	....

Task 15

First enter the data in the spreadsheet, then total the first row using a function. When you have done this, replicate the instruction so that totals appear for the remaining rows in the spreadsheet.

Then use a function to calculate the sum of the first column of figures. Then replicate this function to produce the sum of the remaining columns of figures.

When it is complete, print out the spreadsheet.

```
TASK 15

SALES OF SPORTSWEAR

ITEM            SPRING      SUMMER      AUTUMN      WINTER      TOTAL

Tracksuit         15          30          19          10
Holdall           39          74          26          69
Leotard           55          90          32          85
Culottes          25          55          33          10
Sweatshirt        25          60          20          69
Shorts            33          46          27          70
Swimsuit          34          48          22          13
Trunks            45          59          32          10
Goggles           14          24          10           5
Sunglasses        75          99          32           2

TOTAL
```

Task 16

First enter the data in the spreadsheet, then average the first row using a function. When you have done this, replicate the instruction so that averages appear for the remaining rows in the spreadsheet.

Then use a function to calculate the average for the North. Then replicate this function to produce the average for the remaining regions.

When it is complete, print out the spreadsheet.

TASK 16

PACKETS OF CRISPS SOLD

VARIETY	NORTH	SOUTH	MIDLANDS	WALES	AVERAGE
Plain	1,200	1,500	900	1,100	
Smoky bacon	300	250	1,000	200	
Prawn cocktail	200	180	900	100	
Salt and vinegar	2,000	2,200	1,500	1,900	
Cheese and onion	900	700	200	700	
Oxo	400	250	100	500	
Tomato	150	90	70	50	
Square	700	700	800	1,000	
Low fat	150	600	300	200	

AVERAGE

Task 17

Task 17 gives practice in totalling sums of money. Before you start to enter data in the spreadsheet, make sure that your numeric display allows for two decimal places, so that you can enter both the pounds and pence. You will also need your instructions for totalling and replicating.

(1) Load up your spreadsheet program.

(2) Enter the heading TRAVELLING EXPENSES.

(3) Enter the following headings

NAME   1ST QTR   2ND QTR   3RD QTR   4TH QTR   TOTAL

(4) In the first column enter the following names (left-justified):

Adams
Baker
Callaghan
Jackson
Roberts
Smythe

(5) Enter the data shown below using pounds and pence format:

NAME	1ST QTR	2ND QTR	3RD QTR	4TH QTR	TOTAL
	£	£	£	£	£
Adams	110.50	80.00	125.75	97.50	
Baker	90.00	89.00	102.50	120.00	
Callaghan	223.00	201.50	220.75	215.99	
Jackson	150.00	132.75	149.00	155.00	
Roberts	273.50	208.59	253.95	265.95	
Smythe	84.00	80.00	99.00	83.95	

(6) Add the word TOTAL to the end of column A.

(7) Use a function to calculate the total for the first quarter.

(8) Use the replicate command to copy this function and calculate the totals for the remaining quarters.

(9) Use a function to calculate the total travelling expenses for Adams. Use the replicate command to copy this function and calculate the total expenses for the other people.

(10) Print the spreadsheet.

Saving and retrieving files

When you use a spreadsheet, the information you enter appears on the screen, but, as it is only stored temporarily, it will be lost when the computer is switched off. This means that if you want a permanent record of your work, you must save it on a disk.

When you save work on a disk, it is stored in a **file**. Each file must have its own distinctive name so that it can be found again easily. Once a file is saved on disk, it must be retrieved before you can work on it. If you do fresh work on a file and make changes, you must save your work on disk again, or the changes will be lost.

To complete the next tasks, make sure you know how to save work on disk and retrieve it.

Function	Keystrokes used
Save on disk	....
Retrieve from disk	....

Task 18

Task 18 gives practice in averaging sums of money. Before you start to enter data in the spreadsheet, make sure that your numeric display allows for two decimal places, so that you can enter both the pounds and pence. You will also need your instructions for replicating.

```
TASK  18

ITEM            REGENCY    FARMHOUSE    HI-TECH     PINE    AVERAGE

Base unit        27.00       30.00       35.00     36.00
Wall unit        29.50       33.50       39.50     40.50
Drawer unit      35.00       46.00       66.00     63.00
Carousel         37.99       49.99       70.99     54.99
Broom unit       78.00       83.00       87.00     96.00
Oven housing     49.99       52.99       55.00     60.00
Over hob         46.00       49.00       53.00     54.00
Sink base       100.00      105.00      110.00     99.00
```

When it is complete, save and print your spreadsheet.

Retrieve Task 18 from disk and amend it as shown. When it is correct, save and print it again.

TASK 18

ITEM	REGENCY	FARMHOUSE	HI-TECH	RUSTIC ~~PINE~~	AVERAGE
Base unit	27.00	30.00	35.00	36.00	
Wall unit	29.50	33.50	39.50	40.50	
Drawer unit	35.00	46.00	66.00	63.00	
Corner unit ~~Carousel~~	37.99	49.99	70.99	54.99	
Broom unit	78.00	83.00	87.00	96.00	
Oven casing ~~Oven housing~~	49.99	52.99	55.00	60.00	
Over hob	46.00	49.00	53.00	54.00	
Sink base	100.00	105.00	110.00	99.00	
Open corner	30.00	34.50	40.50	41.50	
Display unit	38.00	49.00	69.50	66.00	
TOTAL					

Task 19

(1) Load your spreadsheet program.

(2) Enter the heading TABLEWARE.

(3) Enter the following column headings:
ITEM CARNIVAL CHINOIS ELEGANCE FLEUR AVERAGE

(4) In the first column enter the following (left-justified):
Tea cup
Saucer
Bowl
Tea plate
Dinner plate

(5) Enter the data shown below:

ITEM	CARNIVAL	CHINOIS	ELEGANCE	FLEUR	AVERAGE
Tea cup	1.75	2.99	4.00	2.00	
Saucer	1.25	2.50	3.48	1.50	
Bowl	2.00	3.50	4.00	3.50	
Tea plate	1.50	3.00	3.48	1.75	
Dinner plate	3.00	4.99	6.48	3.99	

(6) Change the name CARNIVAL to CARIBBEAN, and CHINOIS to ORIENTAL.

(7) Add another row at the end of the spreadsheet with the following entries:
Teapot 3.50 5.00 7.00 4.50

(8) Use a function to calculate the average price for a tea cup.

(9) Then use the replicate command to copy this function and calculate the average for the remaining items of tableware.

(10) Save and print your spreadsheet.

(11) Retrieve Task 19 from disk and amend it as shown. When it is correct, save and print it again.

TASK 19

ITEM	CARIBBEAN	ORIENTAL	ELEGANCE	BLOSSOM ~~FLEUR~~	AVERAGE
Tea cup	1.75	2.99	4.00	2.00	
Saucer	1.25	2.50	3.48	1.50	
Bowl	2.00	3.50	4.00	3.50	
Side plate ~~Tea plate~~	1.50	3.00	3.48	1.75	
Dinner plate	3.00	4.99	6.48	3.99	
Teapot	3.50	5.00	7.00	4.50	
Milk jug	2.00	3.50	4.00	3.50	
Sugar bowl	1.90	3.20	4.50	2.50	
TOTAL					

Task 20 – top of the class spreadsheet

For Task 20, set up a spreadsheet for the test or assignment marks for the students in your class.

Give your spreadsheet a title, such as **STUDENT GRADES**, and put in headings like those shown below:

NAME   TEST 1   TEST 2   TEST 3   FINAL EXAM   AVERAGE

In the column **NAME**, enter the names of everyone in your class (in alphabetical order).

Now put in marks for each student's performance in the tests, and use the replicate command to calculate each student's average mark. Also calculate the average mark for each test.

The layout of the spreadsheet should look like the one shown below.

STUDENT GRADES

NAME	TEST 1	TEST 2	TEST 3	FINAL EXAM	AVERAGE
Carson J	50	55	63	52	
Davies L	40	56	53	55	
Hall M	65	62	66	65	
Knight T	25	38	39	40	
Robertson A	74	72	68	70	
Steele B	61	55	59	63	
AVERAGE					

Save the spreadsheet on disk and print out a copy.

Recall the spreadsheet and alter it to read **TOTAL** instead of **AVERAGE**. Use a function and the replicate command to calculate the total marks for each student and the total marks for each test.

The layout of the spreadsheet should have been altered as shown below.

STUDENT GRADES

NAME	TEST 1	TEST 2	TEST 3	FINAL EXAM	TOTAL
Carson J	50	55	63	52	
Davies L	40	56	53	55	
Hall M	65	62	66	65	
Knight T	25	38	39	40	
Robertson A	74	72	68	70	
Steele B	61	55	59	63	
TOTAL					

Check that the last column and row have been automatically recalculated following these changes, and print out the spreadsheet again.

More advanced calculations

In Unit 3 you will use formulae to perform calculations. A **formula** is an instruction which you write yourself. Unlike a function, it is not a ready-made instruction provided by the spreadsheet, so what the instruction is depends on what you are trying to achieve.

Formulae can also be replicated (copied), altered and printed out, and in this unit you will concentrate on all these things.

- ■ Writing a formula

- ■ Replicating and recalculating a formula

- ■ Printing out a formula

Writing a formula

A formula gives an instruction to perform a certain type of calculation, and the most common of these are:

> Addition
> Subtraction
> Multiplication
> Division

Sometimes, you can have a formula that is very complicated and performs several of these calculations together, but in this unit you will only be writing fairly simple formulae.

In the example below, the formula has been written to give the profit made by a company by subtracting expenses (shown here in cell B5) from sales (shown here in cell B4).

	A	B	C	D	E	F
1	SUPER SPORTS LTD					
2		January	February	March	April	
3						
4	Sales	6500.00	5000.00	7100.00	10500.00	
5	Expenses	1500.00	1000.00	2100.00	2500.00	
6						
7	Profit	5000.00				

B7 B4–B5

Formula   Result of the formula shown in cell B7

■ *Replicating formulae*

Like functions, formulae can be replicated. You should find out how to do this and make a note of the keystrokes used.

Function	Keystrokes used
Formula for addition	....
Formula for subtraction	....
Replication of a formula	....

Task 21

In Task 21 you will be writing a formula for adding the contents of cells together. In the past, you have done this using the function for producing a total, but this time, you are going to practise writing your own formula.

The column on the right-hand side gives a running total for petty cash expenses, and you will be expected to add to it each time a payment is made from petty cash. The formula you write will be based on the calculation:

Previous running total + Stationery/Fares/Misc = Running total

When you have completed the spreadsheet, and have the total spent in November, print it out.

```
TASK 21

PETTY CASH PAYMENTS

DATE       STATIONERY      FARES     MISCELLANEOUS      RUNNING TOTAL

1 Nov                                                        00.00
7 Nov         9.50
12 Nov                     5.00          4.25
14 Nov        1.40         2.00
15 Nov                     1.25          3.00
17 Nov                     2.00
18 Nov        3.00         1.00
23 Nov        0.99                      10.00
24 Nov                     7.30          2.99
27 Nov        7.30                       5.50
28 Nov                                   0.75
30 Nov        6.95
```

Task 22

In Task 22 you will be writing a formula for subtracting the contents of one cell from another. You are going to practise writing your own formula, but when you have done this, it can be replicated in the PROFIT column to complete the spreadsheet more quickly.

The column on the right-hand side gives the profit for each month, and the calculation you will be expected to make is:

Sales – Expenses = Profit

When you have completed the spreadsheet, including the PROFIT column, print it out.

```
TASK 22

MONTH              SALES      EXPENSES      PROFIT

January          1200.00        350.00
February          950.00        125.00
March            1555.00        290.00
April            1350.00        500.00
May               900.00        340.00
June             2600.00       1250.00
July             3530.00        250.00
August           6400.00        330.00
September        5200.00        125.00
October           940.00        125.00
November          820.00        125.00
December          670.00        125.00
```

Task 23

In Task 23 you will also be writing a formula for subtracting the contents of one cell from another. You are going to practise writing your own formula, but when you have done this, it can be replicated in the **NET PAY** column to complete the spreadsheet more quickly.

The column on the right-hand side gives the net pay for each person, and the calculation you will be expected to make is:

Gross pay – (Tax + National Insurance) = Net pay

When you have completed the spreadsheet, print it out.

```
TASK 23

NAME            GROSS PAY           TAX             NI          NET PAY

Anderson  J      1928.00          547.00         106.00
Baring  P        1500.00          398.00          87.00
Dean  A          1256.00          314.00          85.00
French  E         987.00          248.00          80.00
Gough  L         2053.00          549.00          96.00
Hawkins  C        524.00          131.00          56.00
Jennings  G       392.00           98.00          39.00
Philips  H       3690.00          923.00         160.00
Stephens  M       742.00          186.00          68.00
Wilson  F         850.00          212.00          73.00
```

Task 24

In Task 24 you will also be writing a formula for subtracting the contents of one cell from another. You are going to practise writing your own formula, but when you have done this, it can be replicated in the row entitled **CASH FLOW** to complete the spreadsheet more quickly.

The row entitled **SALES** gives the total income for each month, and that entitled **TOTAL EXPENSES** gives the outgoings for each month. First you must total the expenses (you can use a function for this), then the calculation you will be expected to make is:

Sales – Total expenses = Cash flow

When you have completed the spreadsheet, print it out.

TASK 24

KELLY'S BAKERY
Quarterly cash flow

	October	November	December
SALES	16,400.00	15,500.00	13,900.00
EXPENSES			
Shop rental	1,200.00	1,200.00	1,200.00
Utilities	1,000.00	1,100.00	1,150.00
Phone	92.00	86.00	130.00
Salaries	1,050.00	1,050.00	1,350.00
Advertising	750.00	820.00	930.00
Cost of goods	3,856.00	3,739.00	4,493.00
TOTAL EXPENSES			
CASH FLOW			

Function	Keystrokes used
Formula for multiplication	....
Formula for division	....
Replication of a formula	....

Task 25

In Task 25 you will be writing a formula for multiplying the contents of cells together. As you have not used multiplication in a spreadsheet before, you must make sure you understand what keystroke to use for the multiplication sign before you try to write your own formula.

You are going to calculate the cost of hotel accommodation in Devon, and you must write the formula from the calculation:

Price per night × Number of nights = Hotel cost.

Once you have written the formula for the first hotel, you can replicate it to work out the cost for all the other hotels.

When you have completed the spreadsheet, print it out.

```
TASK 25

LOCATION          HOTEL           PER NIGHT      NIGHTS      COST

Lynton            Sandpiper         35.00          3
Combe Martin      Manor House       20.00          2
Ilfracombe        Watersmeet        42.00          4
Braunton          The Crown         15.50          2
Barnstaple        Northfield        28.00          2
South Molton      White House       16.00          4
Oakford           Hunter's Inn      14.95          5
Tiverton          Royal Oak         20.00          2
Twitchen          The Anchor        32.00          3
Parracombe        Ship Inn          38.50          4
```

Task 26

In Task 26 you will also be writing a formula for multiplying the contents of cells together.

You are going to calculate the cost of carpeting a house, and you must write the formula from the calculation:

Price per sq metre × Number of sq metres = Cost of carpet

Once you have written the formula for the first room, you can replicate it to work out the cost for all the other rooms in the house.

When you have completed the spreadsheet, print it out.

TASK 26

ROOM	CARPET	PRICE PER SQ METRE	NO OF SQ METRES	COST
Lounge	Axminster	30.00	16	
Dining room	Stainmaster	25.00	14	
Study	Berber	18.99	9	
Hallway	Patterned	15.99	14	
Stairs	Patterned	15.99	18	
Landing	Twist pile	12.95	8	
Main bedroom	Velvet pile	20.99	15	
Bedroom 2	Saxony	25.00	12	
Guest room	Tonal	18.99	9	
Nursery	Sculptured	14.99	9	

In Task 27 you will be writing a formula for dividing the contents of one cell by that of another cell. As you have not used division in a spreadsheet before, you must make sure you understand what keystroke to use for the division sign before you try to write your own formula.

You are going to calculate the time it takes to travel to different destinations when the average speed per hour varies because of road conditions. You must write the formula from the calculation:

Distance ÷ Speed = Travel time

Once you have written the formula for the first destination, you can replicate it to work out the time for all the other destinations.

When you have completed the spreadsheet, print it out.

TASK 27

DESTINATION	DISTANCE	SPEED	TIME (HOURS)
Brighton	53	50	
Bristol	120	65	
Carlisle	307	50	
Dover	78	45	
Edinburgh	405	49	
Holyhead	267	51	
Inverness	564	48	
Liverpool	211	62	
Maidstone	37	40	
Manchester	199	61	

Task 28

In Task 28 you will also be writing a formula for dividing the contents of one cell by that of another cell.

You are going to calculate the estimated time it takes to complete different building jobs when the numbers of workers allocated to each job varies. You must write the formula from the calculation:

Man hours ÷ Number of workers = Estimated time

Once you have written the formula for the first building job, you can replicate it to work out the time for all the other building jobs.

When you have completed the spreadsheet, print it out.

```
TASK 28

JOB                    MAN HOURS        WORKERS      ESTIMATED TIME

20 ft wall                   92            2
Double garage               108            4
Garden patio                 90            3
Lounge extension            210           12
Granny flat                 320           10
Re-roofing                 1050            9
Fitted kitchen              900            7
Underpinning               1230           10
Swimming pool               210            3
Loft conversion             365            4
```

Printing out a formula and recalculation

In the remaining tasks in this unit you will be required to print out the formulae that you have written (if your software permits this) and also recalculate the figures produced.

Recalculations are done automatically on many spreadsheets. However, you may find you have to do them manually, or you may be able to select either option.

Function	Keystrokes used
Print out a formula	....
Select automatic recalculation	....
Select manual recalculation	....

Task 29

(1) Load up your spreadsheet program.

(2) Enter the heading INVOICE.

(3) Enter the following headings:
REF   ITEM   QUANTITY   UNIT PRICE   TOTAL

(4) In the first column enter the following as labels left-justified:
```
B725
F890
S633
P910
J245
P980
F896
S631
J246
B724
```

(5) Enter the data shown below:

REF	ITEM	QUANTITY	UNIT PRICE	TOTAL
B725	Gents blazer	200	150.00	
F890	Track suit	370	45.00	
S633	Sweater	1200	20.99	
P910	Running shorts	980	12.00	
J245	T-shirt	2300	9.99	
P980	Trunks	400	16.50	
F896	Sweatshirt	120	9.50	
S631	Slip over	50	12.99	
J246	Sun visor	90	2.50	
B724	Anorak	350	49.50	

(6) Write a formula to calculate the total price of the items ordered and print it out.

(7) Then use the replicate command to copy this formula and calculate the total price for the remaining items on the spreadsheet.

(8) When it is complete, save the spreadsheet on disk and print it out.

(9) Retrieve Task 29 from disk and, selecting automatic recalculation, make amendments as shown.

```
TASK 29

REF          ITEM            QUANTITY     UNIT PRICE     TOTAL
                                            50.00
B725      Cagoule             200         150.00
          Gents blazer

F890      Track suit          370          45.00

S633      Sweater            1200          20.99
                             720
P910      Running shorts      980          12.00

J245      T-shirt            2300           9.99

P980      Trunks              400          16.50

F896      Sweatshirt          120           9.50
                             25
S631      Slip over           50           12.99

D912                                         1.95
J246      Sun visor           90            2.50

B724      Anorak             350           49.50
```

(10) When the amendments are complete, write a formula and double all the figures in the **QUANTITY** column. The column for **TOTAL** should be adjusted automatically.

(11) Then save the spreadsheet again and print it out.

Task 30

(1) Load up your spreadsheet program.

(2) Enter the heading TRUSTY CAR PARTS LTD.

(3) Enter the following headings:
ITEM REF PRICE IN NO IN STOCK PRICE OUT PROFIT

(4) In the first column enter the following as labels left-justified:
54100
54101
54102
54103
54104
54105
54106
54107
54108

(5) Enter the data shown below:

ITEM REF	PRICE IN	NO IN STOCK	PRICE OUT	PROFIT
54100	3.99	20	4.50	
54101	5.50	20	6.00	
54102	2.00	20	2.55	
54103	7.25	20	8.00	
54104	2.20	20	3.10	
54105	1.00	20	2.15	
54106	4.30	20	5.45	
54107	0.99	20	1.90	
54108	6.50	20	7.35	

(6) Write a formula to calculate the profit on the items in stock. Base this on the calculation

Price out – Price in = Profit

Print the formula out.

(7) Then use the replicate command to copy this formula and calculate the total profit for the remaining items on the spreadsheet.

(8) When the spreadsheet is complete, save it on disk and print it out.

(9) Retrieve Task 30 from disk and, selecting automatic recalculation, make amendments as shown.

TASK 30

ITEM REF	PRICE IN	NO IN STOCK	PRICE OUT	PROFIT
54100	3.99	20	4.50	
54101	5.25 ~~5.50~~	20	6.00	
54102	2.00	20	2.55	
54103	7.25	20	8.20 ~~8.00~~	
54104	2.20	20	3.10	
54105	1.00	20	1.85 ~~2.15~~	
54106	4.30	20	5.45	
54107	1.10 ~~0.99~~	20	1.90	
54108	6.50	20	7.35	
54109	5.00	20	6.00	
54110	2.90	20	3.20	

---

(10) When the amendments are complete, add another column on the right-hand side entitled STOCK VALUE. Write a formula to calculate the value of the stock; base this on the calculation

Price in × No in stock = Stock value

(11) Then write a formula to halve all the figures in the NO IN STOCK column. The STOCK VALUE column should be automatically recalculated.

(12) When it is complete, save the spreadsheet again and print it out.

Task 31 – bank balance spreadsheet

In Task 31 you are going to concentrate on setting up your own monthly bank statement. If you do not have one of your own to copy from, you can take items from the suggested statement below, and alter them as you choose.

First give your spreadsheet a heading, such as STATEMENT OF ACCOUNT. Then enter column headings as follows:

DATE   ITEM   CREDIT   DEBIT   BALANCE

You can enter suitable dates for yourself (using the day and month only) to cover a one-month period. This need not start with the first day of the month. Below is a suggestion covering a month from 7 November to 7 December.

```
7-11
12-11
13-11
19-11
22-11
23-11
30-11
3-12
4-12
4-12
7-12
```

Enter data such as that shown below. Notice that the statement must start with the balance (i.e. the sum of money) you have in your bank account on the first day that the statement refers to.

DATE	ITEM	CREDIT	DEBIT	BALANCE
7-11	Brought fwd			1010.50
12-11	Mortgage		554.00	
13-11	Water rates		18.18	
19-11	Cash		50.00	
22-11	Cheque	320.00		
23-11	Community charge		33.80	
30-11	Salary	1350.50		
3-12	Cheque		149.50	
4-12	Cash		50.00	
4-12	Cheque	85.00		
7-12	Carried fwd			

Write a formula to calculate the balance after the first debit, and print out this formula.

Then use the replicate command to copy this formula and calculate the balance for the rest of the statement.

When the spreadsheet is complete, save it on disk and print it out.

Retrieve the spreadsheet from disk and selecting automatic recalculation, make some amendments like those shown. Obviously, they do not have to be the same amendments, but you should practise making alterations and checking to see that the balance has been altered too.

DATE	ITEM	CREDIT	DEBIT	BALANCE
7-11	Brought fwd			1010.50
12-11	Mortgage		475.00 ~~554.00~~	
13-11	Water rates		18.18	
19-11	Auto service ~~Cash~~		50.00	
22-11	Cheque	120.00 ~~320.00~~		
23-11	Community charge		33.80	
30-11	Salary	1350.50		
3-12	Direct debit ~~Cheque~~		149.50	
4-12	Cash		50.00	
4-12	Cheque	85.00		
7-12	Carried fwd			

When the amendments are complete, write a formula to halve all the figures in the DEBIT column. The column for the BALANCE should be adjusted automatically.

Then save the spreadsheet again and print it out.

Revising a spreadsheet

In Unit 4 you will practise making large-scale alterations to the layout of your spreadsheet. So far, you have learnt to correct a spreadsheet by erasing single cells or by performing recalculations.

You may want to revise your spreadsheet for several reasons. If you are not satisfied by its appearance you may want to alter it, so that the display is improved and it is easier to understand. Alternatively, you may find it quicker to make alterations to an old spreadsheet, rather than produce a new one from scratch.

In this unit you will concentrate on:

- Deletions
- Insertions
- Moving and copying
- Erasing the spreadsheet

Deleting rows and columns

It is possible to delete entire columns and entire rows from a spreadsheet if the information they contain is no longer needed.

When you delete a column, all the columns to the right of it will move across so that no gap is left on the spreadsheet. Similarly, when you delete a row, all the rows beneath it will move up so that no gap is left.

	A	B	C	D	E	F
1	Item	January	February	March		
2						
3	Nails	22,270	20,195	24,860		
4	Hinges	7,294	7,520	8,143		
5	Nuts	8,425	7.694	9,625		
6	Bolts	39,500	38,770	42,838		
7						

Rows to be deleted

	A	B	C	D	E	F
1	Item	January	February	March		
2						
3	Nails	22,270	20,195	24,860		
4	Bolts	39,500	38,770	42,838		
5						

Spreadsheet after deleting the rows

Function	Keystrokes used
Delete one or more columns	....
Delete one or more rows	....

Task 32

In Task 32 you must enter the spreadsheet as it is shown and print it out. Then, you must delete two separate columns on the spreadsheet, the column for COLOUR and the column for ORIGIN. If you do this correctly, there will be no gaps left, and GEMSTONE will become column A, and Q1 will become column B.

When the deletions are complete, print out the spreadsheet again.

TASK 32

HARRIS JEWELLERS
Quarterly sales of gemstones

COLOUR	GEMSTONE	ORIGIN	Q1	Q2	Q3	Q4
Purple	Amethyst	Brazil	340	297	189	372
Yellow	Citrine	Malawi	142	165	193	108
White	Diamond	S Africa	792	841	677	743
Green	Emerald	Thailand	250	296	287	264
Red	Garnet	India	590	585	463	421
Green	Jade	China	98	87	65	46
Green	Peridot	Botswana	26	38	29	45
Red	Ruby	Burma	108	194	173	126
Blue	Sapphire	Sri Lanka	460	412	438	322
White	Zircon	Uruguay	38	46	31	29

Task 33

In Task 33 you must enter the spreadsheet as it is shown, total up the columns and rows in the budget and print it out.

Then, you must delete two separate rows on the spreadsheet – the row for **Hairdressing** and the row for **Newspapers**. If you do this correctly, there will be no gaps left.

When the deletions are complete and the totals have been adjusted, print out the spreadsheet again.

TASK 33

PERSONAL BUDGET

TYPE	ACCOUNT	OCT	NOV	DEC	TOTAL
Clothes	Current	20	30	90	
Hairdressing	Current	14	0	25	
Housekeeping	Current	150	150	180	
Mortgage	Current	230	230	230	
Insurance	Current	20	20	20	
Newspapers	Current	3	3	7	
Petrol	Current	14	14	14	
Savings	Deposit	45	40	12	
Going out	Current	23	39	46	
Snacks	Current	5	5	5	
Holidays	Deposit	28	36	7	
Miscellaneous	Current	29	24	28	
TOTAL					

Task 34

In Task 34 you must enter the spreadsheet as it is shown, and total the timber exports. Next, write a formula for the profit based on the calculation:

Total exports – Timber imports = Profit

Then print out the spreadsheet.

Next, you must delete the column **PURPOSE** on the spreadsheet, and the two rows entitled **Juniper** and **Lime**. The total exports and profit must also be recalculated.

When the deletions are complete and the totals have been adjusted, print out the spreadsheet again.

```
TASK 34

TIMBER TRADING PROFITS

IMPORTS           PURPOSE         PREVIOUS          CURRENT
                                      YEAR             YEAR
                                   7900.00          9500.00
                                 _____      _____

EXPORTS
Alder             Cabinets          120.00           152.00
Ash               Stakes           8840.00          9325.00
Beech             Fences            732.00           695.00
Cherry            Furniture         850.00           895.00
Fir               Poles            6300.00          5980.00
Juniper           Pencils           281.00           362.00
Lime              Pianos            971.00           824.00
Oak               Furniture        9120.00          9740.00
Poplar            Boxes            5210.00          5500.00
Spruce            Paper            9400.00          9670.00
Yew               Posts             645.00           532.00

TOTAL EXPORTS

PROFIT
```

Inserting columns and rows

As you work on a spreadsheet you may find that you want to insert new columns or rows. The reason for this may be purely to enhance the appearance of the spreadsheet by leaving more space, or it may be because extra information must be inserted.

When new columns or rows are inserted, they are always empty. Fresh information can then be entered in the empty cells.

	A	B	C	D	E	F
1	Item	January	February	March		
2						
3	Nails	22,270	20,195	24,860		
4	Hinges	7,294	7,520	8,143		
5	Nuts	8,425	7.694	9,625		
6	Bolts	39,500	38,770	42,838		
7						

The spreadsheet before inserting a row

	A	B	C	D	E	F
1	Item	January	February	March		
2						
3	Nails	22,270	20,195	24,860		
4	Hinges	7,294	7,520	8,143		
5						
6	Nuts	8,425	7.694	9,625		
7	Bolts	39,500	38,770	42,838		
8						

The spreadsheet after inserting a row

	A	B	C	D	E	F
1	Item	January	February	March		
2						
3	Nails	22,270	20,195	24,860		
4	Hinges	7,294	7,520	8,143		
5	Locks	954	872	983		
6	Nuts	8,425	7.694	9,625		
7	Bolts	39,500	38,770	42,838		
8						

Fresh information has been entered in the empty cells

In Task 35 you must enter the spreadsheet as it is shown, and calculate the price for the items using the formula:

Quantity × Unit price = Total price

You must also total the whole invoice and then print it out.

When this has been done, insert a column on the spreadsheet after DESCRIPTION and enter the following information:

COLOUR
Barley
Harvest
Off white
Off white
Ice
Gardenia
Teak
Dark matt
Evergreen
Natural

When the insertions are complete, print out the spreadsheet again.

```
TASK 35

PAINT ORDER

DESCRIPTION          QUANTITY        UNIT PRICE        TOTAL PRICE

Matt emulsion           15              6.99
Silk emulsion           27              6.50
Undercoat                9              5.50
Wood primer             12              4.95
Gloss                   12              6.25
Masonry paint          100             11.50
Wood stain               5             12.30
Varnish                  8              7.90
Timber paint            14              4.99
Preservative             2              5.20

TOTAL
```

Task 36

In Task 36 you must enter the spreadsheet as it is shown, and calculate the total price for the skiing holidays in Scotland and France. Then print out the spreadsheet.

When this has been done, insert an empty row on the spreadsheet after **BASIC COST**. Insert another row after **Lessons** with the following information:

Lunches   20.00   38.00

and another row after **Ski lift** with the following information:

Snacks   9.00   14.00

Make sure that the total cost has been recalculated and print out the spreadsheet again.

```
TASK 36

COMPARATIVE COSTS

                    SCOTLAND        FRANCE

BASIC COST           125.00         200.00

EXTRAS
   Discos              9.00           9.00
   Drinks             10.00           8.00
   Excursions         21.00          25.00
   Lessons            52.00          85.00
   Ski hire           23.00          49.00
   Ski lift           14.00          36.00
   Tips                5.00          17.00
   Transport           8.00          00.00

TOTAL COST
```

In Task 37 you must enter the spreadsheet as it is shown, and calculate the total expenses for each sales manager, and the average cost incurred for hotel accommodation, transport and entertaining. Then print out the spreadsheet.

When this has been done, insert a row on the spreadsheet after **Miller K** with the following information:

Naughton S   250.00   110.00   62.00

Then insert a column between **TRANSPORT** and **ENTERTAINING** with the following information:

PHONE
23.00
19.00
 3.00
35.00
 2.50
19.89
 7.80
40.00
 5.00
16.50

Make sure the total expenses and average costs are recalculated and print out the spreadsheet again.

TASK 37

MANAGERS' EXPENSES

MANAGER	HOTEL	TRANSPORT	ENTERTAINING	TOTAL
Baker J	300.00	102.00	90.00	
Burton D	549.00	240.00	150.00	
Collins G	90.00	25.00	52.00	
Evans P	87.00	15.00	20.00	
Jones A	140.00	50.00	33.00	
Miller K	89.00	20.00	14.00	
Stevens M	290.00	180.00	136.00	
Thompson B	168.00	52.00	74.00	
Walton A	95.00	30.00	14.00	
Williams C	200.00	109.00	114.00	

AVERAGE

■ *Moving and copying entries*

Entries on a spreadsheet may be moved in order to improve the display and make it clearer and easier to understand. Any entry can be moved – labels (text), values (figures) or formulae. When an entry is moved, it will *only* appear in its new location.

	A	B	C	D	E	F
1	MEAT SALES					
2						
3	TYPE	WEEK 1	WEEK 2			
4	Pork	134.00	101.00			
5	Beef	300.00	350.00			
6	Lamb	98.00	84.00			

Entries before being moved

	A	B	C	D	E	F
1	MEAT SALES					
2						
3	TYPE	WEEK 1	WEEK 2			
4						
5	Beef	300.00	350.00			
6	Lamb	98.00	84.00			
7	Pork	134.00	101.00			

Entries after being moved

Entries on a spreadsheet may be copied if they need to be duplicated elsewhere. Copying saves the chore of re-entering information cell by cell. Any entry can be copied – labels (text), values (figures) or formulae. When an entry is copied, it will appear *both* in its old location and its new location.

	A	B	C	D	E	F
1		NOVEMBER	SALES	DECEMBER	SALES	
2	ITEM	SHOP 1	SHOP 2			
3	Sweets	250.00	280.00			
4	Chocolates	68.00	91.00			
5	Ice cream	36.00	44.00			

Entries before being copied

	A	B	C	D	E	F
1		NOVEMBER	SALES	DECEMBER	SALES	
2	ITEM	SHOP 1	SHOP 2	SHOP 1	SHOP 2	
3	Sweets	250.00	280.00			
4	Chocolates	68.00	91.00			
5	Ice cream	36.00	44.00			

Entries after being copied

Function	Keystrokes used
Move entry	....
Copy entry	....

Task 38

In Task 38 you must enter the spreadsheet as it is shown, and calculate the average marks for each student. Then print out the spreadsheet.

When this has been done, move the details of all the students who have failed one or both of the tests down to the end of the list, deleting any empty rows that are left. Then calculate the average marks for the first test and the second test and print out the spreadsheet again.

TASK 38

NAME	TEST 1	RESULT	TEST 2	RESULT	AVERAGE
Atkins P	50	Pass	53	Pass	
Billings M	43	Fail	40	Fail	
Coulson A	40	Fail	55	Pass	
Erikson B	75	Credit	73	Credit	
Fyfield B	64	Pass	69	Pass	
Grigsby D	58	Pass	48	Fail	
Hawton J	56	Pass	55	Pass	
Hirani D	70	Credit	68	Pass	
Mehri J	39	Fail	47	Fail	
Patel R	61	Pass	57	Pass	
Roberts T	51	Pass	52	Pass	
Vernon M	56	Pass	55	Pass	

In Task 39 you must enter the spreadsheet as it is shown, and and copy the details of expenses for the seven-day holiday on the Costa Brava down to the Adriatic and to Brittany. You must also copy the headings:

LOW SEASON   MID SEASON   HIGH SEASON

down to each resort. When this is done, total the cost of the holidays at each different time of the year, then print out the spreadsheet.

TASK 39

COSTA BRAVA	LOW SEASON	MID SEASON	HIGH SEASON
Accommodation	98.00	130.00	170.00
Return coach	41.00	50.00	55.00
Lunches	40.00	45.00	60.00
Spending money	100.00	110.00	125.00
TOTAL			
ADRIATIC			
	115.00	140.00	180.00
	54.00	59.00	64.00
	45.00	50.00	65.00
	100.00	115.00	130.00
BRITTANY			
	120.00	145.00	190.00
	40.00	45.00	50.00
	43.00	52.00	63.00
	110.00	120.00	130.00

Erasing a spreadsheet from screen

A spreadsheet can be erased from screen if it is incorrect or if there is no use for it any more. If this is done, the cells will be left empty so that new data can be entered in them.

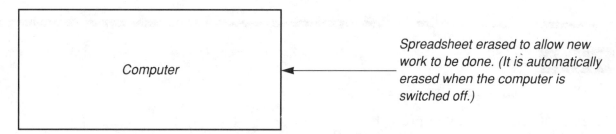

Erasing a spreadsheet from disk

A spreadsheet can be saved as a file on disk and retrieved later for use. If new work is done on the spreadsheet, it must be saved again on disk and the original file must be overwritten. If the file is not required any more, it can be erased from disk.

Saving and retrieving

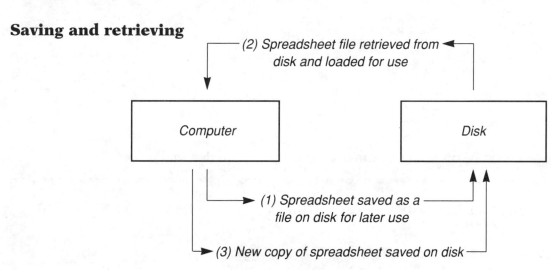

Saving and erasing

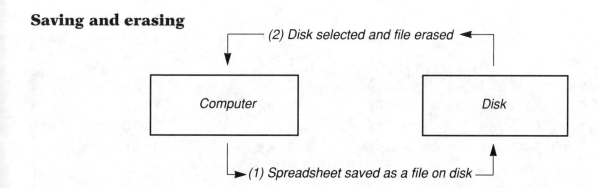

Function	Keystrokes used
Erase spreadsheet from disk	....

Task 40

(1) Load your spreadsheet program.

(2) Enter the title of the spreadsheet:
   `GROCERY LIST COMPARISON`

(3) Starting from the second column, enter the following headings:
   `CHECKIN    SUPASAVE    BUYRITE    FRESHFAYRE`

(4) In the first column enter the following titles (left-justified):
   `Apples`
   `Bacon`
   `Bread`
   `Butter`
   `Coffee`
   `Eggs`
   `Pork chops`
   `Teabags`
   `Tomatoes`
   `Sugar`

(5) Enter the data shown below using a numeric format with two decimal places.

	CHECKIN	SUPASAVE	BUYRITE	FRESHFAYRE	AVG
Apples	1.65	1.45	1.48	1.54	
Bacon	2.37	2.42	2.39	2.65	
Bread	0.52	0.49	0.48	0.52	
Butter	0.65	0.54	0.62	0.69	
Coffee	1.69	1.68	1.69	1.72	
Eggs	1.28	1.25	1.27	1.30	
Pork chops	2.35	2.33	2.36	2.35	
Teabags	1.79	1.77	1.82	1.80	
Tomatoes	0.89	0.85	0.90	0.90	
Sugar	0.66	0.66	0.65	0.66	
TOTAL					

(6) Check your spreadsheet carefully, then calculate the average price of each item bought.

(7) Total the grocery list for each of the four different supermarkets.

(8) Insert an empty row between the names of the supermarkets and the first grocery item (apples).

(9) Insert another empty row between the last item (sugar) and the total.

(10) Save the spreadsheet on disk and print it out.

(11) Retrieve Task 40 and amend it as shown. Make sure that the average and total are recalculated, then print it out. Finally, erase it from disk.

TASK 40

SUPERMARKET
~~GROCERY LIST~~ COMPARISON

	CHECKIN	SUPASAVE	PRICERITE ~~BUYRITE~~	FRESHFAYRE	AVG
Apples	1.65	1.45	1.48	1.54	
Bacon	2.37	2.36 ~~2.42~~	2.39	2.65	
Bread	0.52	0.49	0.50 ~~0.48~~	0.52	
Butter	0.65	0.54	0.62	0.69	
~~Cheddar~~ Coffee	~~2.05~~ 1.69	~~2.00~~ 1.68	~~2.10~~ 1.69	~~2.12~~ 1.72	
Eggs	1.28	1.25	1.27	1.30	
~~Mushrooms~~ Pork chops	~~1.99~~ 2.35	~~1.70~~ 2.33	~~1.79~~ 2.36	~~1.90~~ 2.35	
Teabags	1.79	1.77	1.82	1.80	
Tomatoes	0.89	0.85	0.90	0.92 ~~0.90~~	
Sugar	0.66	0.66	0.65	0.66	
TOTAL					

Task 41 – personal expenditure spreadsheet

In Task 41, plan a spreadsheet for your own personal expenditure and that of a couple of friends.

Make a list of the income you have each month, such as from your grant and from a Saturday job, then write down all the items you normally spend money on, and try to put them into categories.

Work out how much you spend on each category every month and enter it into your spreadsheet using the 'pounds and pence' format.

Make some more columns in the spreadsheet for your friends, and put in their income and expenditure too.

To get the figure for CASH LEFT OVER, subtract the TOTAL EXPENSES from the TOTAL INCOME. Write your own formula to do this, and when the spreadsheet is complete, print it out.

Below is an example of what your spreadsheet may look like, but you should write your own, and not copy this one.

```
TASK 41


                   Sharon      Andrew     Stephen    Patricia


Weekly grant       100.00      100.00      100.00      100.00
Saturday job        28.00        0.00       20.00        0.00
                   _____

TOTAL INCOME


EXPENSES
Accommodation       55.00       45.00       55.00       40.00
Travel               5.00        8.00       10.00       12.00
Food                20.00       25.00       30.00       29.00
College books       20.00       10.00       25.00       10.00
Clothes              3.00        5.00        2.00        3.00
Going out           10.00        5.00       10.00        5.00
Phone calls          2.00        0.00        5.00        1.00
Magazines and
   newspapers        2.00        1.00        2.00        0.00
                   _____

TOTAL EXPENSES


CASH LEFT OVER
```

What is a database?

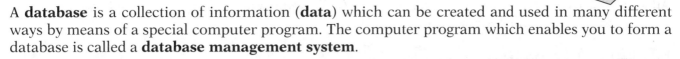

A **database** is a collection of information (**data**) which can be created and used in many different ways by means of a special computer program. The computer program which enables you to form a database is called a **database management system**.

Any sort of information can be collected in a database – names, addresses and phone numbers of customers, sales figures, student records, estate agents' housing lists to give just a few examples. Once the database has been prepared on the computer, it can be manipulated to provide exactly the information that is required.

To enter information in a database, it is necessary to create an **entry form**. This looks like the form people fill in to join a club or apply for a loan. What is different is that the form is designed by the person who is creating the database, and consequently it contains whatever categories are required.

```
FIRST NAME   _____
SURNAME      _____
STUDENT NO   _____
COURSE       _____
```

An example of an entry form

When data has been entered on the entry form it is stored in the database; this has a special structure comprising of columns and rows. A **field** is the name given to the information in each column, and the title of each column is called a **field name**. The entries in each category on the entry form go to make up the different fields of the database.

Field names displayed in the top row

FIRST NAME	SURNAME	STUDENT NO	COURSE
Susan	Carter	92874	Business Administration
Peter	Evans	48355	Computer Literacy
Graham	Wilkins	37662	GCSE

A field

Each row of the database is called a **record**. In other words, a record consists of a single entry from each of the fields (i.e. columns) in the database. All the entries on one entry form go to make up a single record.

FIRST NAME	SURNAME	STUDENT NO	COURSE
Susan	Carter	92874	Business Administration
Peter	Evans	48355	Computer Literacy
Graham	Wilkins	37662	GCSE

A record

Typical features of a database

All databases have common characteristics, though some may be far more sophisticated than others, and may contain many additional features.

Designing and creating an entry form

The different categories on the entry form can be created and laid out to suit the purpose of the user, and the form can be redesigned if it is not satisfactory. The user can decide what types of information are to be entered, and the entry form can specify that an automatic calculation is to be performed, if required.

Editing records

Entries can be viewed one at a time through the entry form, and they can be altered if need be. It is also possible to delete entries, change calculations and remove entire records.

Sorting records

It is a simple matter to change the order in which records have been entered. For example, records can be sorted alphabetically if they contain names, or numerically if sums of money are involved, or even in date order if one of the fields in the record contains a date.

Selecting information

Specific information can be extracted from the database by selecting records. For example, if a database contains names and addresses, it is possible to extract only the names and addresses of those people living in a certain town. It is possible to narrow down the choice of records by making more than one selection.

Printing the database

The entire database can be printed, or only a partial database. This is done either by choosing only certain records to be printed, or by choosing only certain fields.

A typical database would look like this:

Row of field names   Field

CODE NO	DESCRIPTION	PRICE	IN STOCK	REORDER LEVEL
452	Fridge	250.00	10	3
371	Microwave	130.00	25	5
274	Cooker	490.00	5	2
129	Dishwasher	329.00	7	2
590	Freezer	299.00	4	3
583	Tumble drier	159.00	14	4

Cursor   Record

Creating a database

In Unit 5, you are going to design the layout of an entry form and use it to enter records. You will then be able to view the complete database and print it out if you choose. The functions you will learn, apart from printing, are:

■ Creating an entry form

■ Entering records

■ Making changes to records

■ Saving the database

Creating an entry form

An entry form must be designed before it can be created. This means you must decide what **field names** (headings) you want to use for the information. You must also specify what type and length the fields are.

The main **field types** are described below.

Field type	Description
Character	This refers to text and to numbers which are used descriptively.
Number	This includes any number that can be used in a calculation.
Date	This consists of a date.
Calculation	This will contain the result of a calculation and will automatically be entered later.

When you have selected the field types, you must choose the **field lengths**; that is, you must decide the maximum number of characters to allow in each field. This will give you the **specification** for the entry form.

Field name	Field type	Field length
Name	Character	20
Holiday code number	Character	5
Description	Character	25
Date of booking	Date	8
Number of persons	Number	2
Price per person	Number	6
Total amount	Calculation	8

An entry form specification

Once the entry form has been specified, it can be created ready for the records, which make up the database, to be entered.

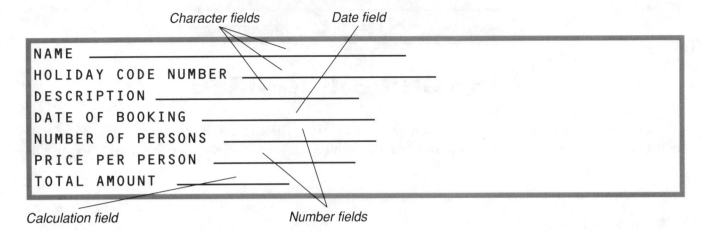

Character fields   Date field

NAME _____
HOLIDAY CODE NUMBER _____
DESCRIPTION _____
DATE OF BOOKING _____
NUMBER OF PERSONS _____
PRICE PER PERSON _____
TOTAL AMOUNT _____

Calculation field   Number fields

Entry form awaiting the first record

■ *Entering records*

After the entry form has been created, the first **record** can be entered. When the entry form is displayed on screen, each field name (heading) is followed by enough space for the corresponding entry to be made.

```
Record 1
NAME     S Harrison
HOLIDAY CODE NUMBER     12445
DESCRIPTION     Pony trekking in Wales
DATE OF BOOKING     19 March
NUMBER OF PERSONS     6
PRICE PER PERSON     150
TOTAL AMOUNT
```

A completed entry form showing the first record

When the first record has been completed and entered, the remaining records should be entered, one by one.

```
Record 2
NAME     J Thornton
HOLIDAY CODE NUMBER     14596
DESCRIPTION     Weekend in Amsterdam
DATE OF BOOKING     23 March
NUMBER OF PERSONS     4
PRICE PER PERSON     130
TOTAL AMOUNT
```

A completed entry form showing the second record

Function	Keystrokes used
Design an entry form	....
Create an entry form	....
Enter a record	....
Correct keying in errors	....
Print the entire database	....

Task 42

Design and create an entry form, using the information given. When the form has been created, enter the data given below and print out the entire database.

Field name	Field type	Field length
Course	Character	15
Code	Character	3
Weeks	Number	2
No of students	Number	2

Information to be entered in the database

TASK 42

COURSE	CODE	WEEKS	NO OF STUDENTS
Drawing	GAB	30	15
Painting	GAC	30	20
Picture framing	GAD	12	12
Carpentry	GAA	30	18
Sculpture	GAJ	30	12
Jewellery	GAE	12	17
Photography	GAI	15	14
Pottery	GAH	30	21
Lino printing	GAF	10	15
Calligraphy	GAG	10	25

Task 43

Design and create an entry form using the information given. When the form has been created, enter the data given below and print out the entire database.

Field name	Field type	Field length
Occupation	Character	15
Name	Character	10
Date of birth (DOB)	Date	8
Insurance	Number	10

Information to be entered in the database

```
TASK 43
OCCUPATION          NAME            DOB             INSURANCE
Nurse               Morris H        10/2/60              120
Teacher             Barnes P        5/9/64               115
Policeman           Levy D          15/6/59              200
Army officer        Patel D         31/3/58              230
Civil servant       Linton M        18/7/61               95
Electrician         Worth J         19/11/55             121
Secretary           Bell T          8/10/65               85
Journalist          Greene A        20/12/47             150
Sales assistant     Cooper B        2/5/43               145
```

Task 44

Design and create an entry form using the information given about hotel accommodation. The field names have been given, but you must decide on the field types and lengths yourself.

When the form has been created, enter the data given below and print out the whole database.

Field name	Field type	Field length
Hotel		
Star rating		
No of beds		
Price per night £		

Information to be entered in the database

```
TASK 44
HOTEL               RATING      NO OF BEDS      PRICE PER NIGHT £
The Railway           3            148                  75
Warwick Hall          4            210                  95
Yardley Lion          2             24                  51
Dickens Inn           4            200                 105
International         4            110                 100
Wayfarer             1             20                  48
Knight at Arms        2             30                  59
Royal Crest           3             56                  77
```

Task 45

Design and create an entry form using the information about software packages. The field names have been given, but you must decide on the field types and lengths yourself.

When the form has been created, enter the data given below and print out the whole database.

Field name	Field type	Field length
Type		
Name		
Stock		
Manufacturer		
Price £		

Information to be entered in the database

```
TASK 45

NAME                    STOCK        MANUFACTURER        PRICE £

WORD PROCESSING
Word Wizard              15          Systems Co             149
Easy Write               12          M G Software            89
Lexicon                  10          Global Ltd             120
Fast Stream              16          Coleman Ltd             99
Style Setter              9          Anglosoft Co           110

GRAPHICS
Fine Art                 14          M G Software            43
Maestro                   8          Global Ltd              57
Firefly                  11          Digisoft Ltd           110

DESKTOP PUBLISHING
Copy Shop                10          Coleman Ltd             89
Paste Up                  8          Digisoft Ltd            56
Legerdemain               7          Anglosoft Co           144
```

Task 46

Design and create an entry form using the information about patients at a health centre. The field names have been given, but you must decide on the field types and lengths yourself.

When the form has been created, enter the data given below and print out the whole database.

Field names
Category (i.e. current, new or referred)
First name
Surname
Date of birth (DOB)
NHS number

Information to be entered in the database

```
TASK 46

FIRST NAME              SURNAME           DOB             NHS NO

CURRENT PATIENTS
Joanna                  Barrington        14/12/70        NHS176
Susan                   Matthews          8/11/63         NHS245
Mark                    Fisher            27/2/54         NHS483
Andrew                  McDonald          12/3/60         NHS128

NEW PATIENTS
Patrick                 Clarkson          5/10/49         NHS693
Sharon                  Bates             31/7/52         NHS271
Lorraine                Harrison          6/8/65          NHS819
Barry                   Shevringham       31/1/71         NHS904

REFERRED PATIENTS
Pamela                  Oakley            17/9/70         NHS732
Balvinder               Grewal            18/9/62         NHS516
Elaine                  Matherson         30/3/55         NHS622
```

Viewing the database

Once you have designed and created the entry form, and keyed in the data, you may wish to view the database to make sure it is correct. It is possible to delete records, add new records and make corrections to existing records.

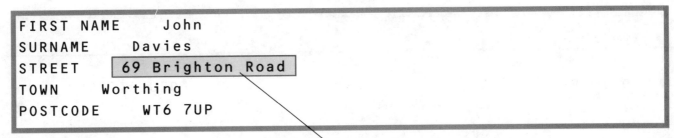

Change of address to be made

Record to be deleted

FIRST NAME	SURNAME	STREET	TOWN	POSTCODE
John	Davies	20 Byron Road	Worthing	WT6 7UP
Marion	Williams	14 Ashby Avenue	Brighton	BR2 9RT
Stephanie	Morland	1 Sidney Street	Crawley	CR3 3LY
Geoffrey	Holmes	134 Garrick Road	Hove	BR4 7HV

New record to be added

FIRST NAME	SURNAME	STREET	TOWN	POSTCODE
John	Davies	69 Brighton Road	Worthing	WT6 7UP
Marion	Williams	14 Ashby Avenue	Brighton	BR2 9RT
Geoffrey	Holmes	134 Garrick Road	Hove	BR4 7HV
Diana	Humphry	2 Overton Walk	Worthing	WT6 7UP

The database before and after alteration

Correcting entries

All corrections are made to the database through the entry form. It does not matter what the correction is – whether it is simply a spelling mistake, or a large-scale alteration – the correction must be still be made on the entry form before it will show in the database.

FIRST NAME	John
SURNAME	Davies
STREET	69 Brighton Road
TOWN	Worthing
POSTCODE	WT6 7UP

Change of address made on the entry form

Deleting records

When the correct record has been selected, it can be deleted, and it will no longer appear when you view the database.

Adding new records

New records can be added by using the entry form, and will be displayed last when you view the database.

Function	Keystrokes used
View the database	....
Correct an entry	....
Delete a record	....
Add a new record	....

Task 47

Design and create an entry form using the information about Australasia. The field names have been given, but you must decide on the field types and lengths yourself.

When the form has been created, enter the data given below and then view the whole database.

Field names
Country
Province
Town
Population

Information to be entered in the database

```
TASK 47

PROVINCE                  TOWN                POPULATION

NEW ZEALAND
North Island              Auckland               149,989
North Island              Wellington             168,000
South Island              Christchurch           247,000

AUSTRALIA
New South Wales           Canberra                92,199
New South Wales           Newcastle              133,967
New South Wales           Sydney               2,444,735
Northern Territory        Alice Springs           11,118
Queensland                Brisbane               719,140
South Australia           Adelaide               809,466
Victoria                  Melbourne            2,108,499
Western Australia         Perth                  465,000
```

When you have viewed the database, make the amendments shown below using the entry form. On completion of the amendments, print out the whole database.

TASK 47

COUNTRY	PROVINCE	TOWN	POPULATION
New Zealand	North Island	Auckland	149,989
New Zealand	North Island	Wellington	168,000
New Zealand	South Island	Christchurch	247,000
Australia	New South Wales	Canberra	92,199
~~Australia~~	~~New South Wales~~	~~Newcastle~~	~~133,967~~
Australia	New South Wales	Sydney	2,444,735
~~Australia~~	~~Northern Territory~~	~~Alice Springs~~	~~11,118~~
Australia	Queensland	Brisbane	719,140
Australia	South Australia	Adelaide	809,466
Australia	Victoria	Melbourne	2,108,499
Australia	Western Australia	Perth	465,000

Delete this record (Newcastle)

Delete this record (Alice Springs)

Add these records:

Australia	Northern Territory	Darwin	14,000
Australia	Tasmania	Hobart	119,415
Australia	Western Australia	Kalgoorlie	21,770

Design and create an entry form using the information about items in different branches of a gift shop. The field names have been given, but you must decide on the field types and lengths yourself.

When the form has been created, enter the data given below (using the abbreviations given for the branches) and then view the whole database.

Field names	Abbreviations
Branch	TC = Town centre
Item	SM = Shopping mall
Material	
Ref no	
Price £	
No in stock	

Information to be entered in the database

TASK 48

ITEM	MATERIAL	REF NO	PRICE £	NO IN STOCK
TOWN CENTRE				
Tankard	Pewter	P21	23	4
Musical box	Wood	W16	12	8
Photo frame	Silver	S48	37	10
Decanter	Crystal	K15	9	3
Money box	China	C30	10	15
SHOPPING MALL				
Vase	Crystal	K14	17	12
Tray	Silver	S47	80	100
Jewel case	Velvet	V21	15	9
Cruet set	Silver	S46	7	10
Fruit bowl	Crystal	K17	30	9

When you have viewed the database, make the amendments shown below using the entry form. On completion of the amendments, print out the whole database.

TASK 48

BRANCH	ITEM	MATERIAL	REF NO	PRICE £	NO IN STOCK
TC	Tankard	Pewter	P21	23	4
TC	Musical box	Wood	W16	12	~~8~~ 3
TC	Photo frame	Silver	S48	37	10
~~TC~~	~~Decanter~~	~~Crystal~~	~~K15~~	~~9~~	~~3~~

Delete this record

TC SM	Money box	~~China~~ Wood	~~C30~~ W15	10	15
SM	Vase	Crystal	K14	17	12
SM	Tray	Silver	S47	~~80~~ 66	100
SM	Jewel case	Velvet	V21	15	9
~~SM~~	~~Cruet set~~	~~Silver~~	~~S46~~	~~7~~	~~10~~

Delete this record

SM	Fruit bowl	Crystal	K17	~~30~~ 45	9

Design and create an entry form using the information about a building society's branches in south-west England. The field names have been given, but you must decide on the field types and lengths yourself.

When the form has been created, enter the data given below (using the abbreviations given for the areas) and then view the whole database.

Field names	Abbreviations
Area	
Location	C = Cornwall
No of offices	D = Devon
No of staff	S = Somerset
No of accounts	

Information to be entered in the database

TASK 49

LOCATION	NO OF OFFICES	NO OF STAFF	NO OF ACCOUNTS
CORNWALL			
Truro	5	25	2264
Redruth	2	10	1539
Camborne	1	9	932
Penzance	2	20	1526
DEVON			
Plymouth	8	50	2679
Exeter	7	42	2458
Torquay	3	20	992
SOMERSET			
Taunton	6	32	2343
Yeovil	3	18	1874
Bridgwater	5	30	2244

When you have viewed the database, make the amendments shown below using the entry form. On completion of the amendments, print out the whole database.

TASK 49

AREA	LOCATION	NO OF OFFICES	NO OF STAFF	NO OF ACCOUNTS
C	Truro	5	29 ~~25~~	3196 ~~2264~~
C	Redruth	2	10	1539
~~C~~	~~Camborne~~	~~1~~	~~9~~	~~932~~
C	Penzance	2	20	1526
D	Plymouth	8	50	2900 ~~2679~~
D	Exeter	7	42	2458
D	Torquay	3	20	992
S	Taunton	6	35 ~~32~~	2343
S	Yeovil	3	18	1874
S	Bridgwater	5	30	2244

Delete this record *(against Camborne row)*

Add these records:

AREA	LOCATION	NO OF OFFICES	NO OF STAFF	NO OF ACCOUNTS
C	St Austell	2	12	1600
D	Tiverton	1	8	723
S	Minehead	1	10	820

For Task 50, set up your own database to store details about the sort of holidays you would like to go on.

First, you should decide what sort of holiday interests you – you may prefer a seaside holiday, or perhaps you would rather go on walking holidays, or visit foreign cities.

When you have made your choice of holiday, list the destinations you would like to visit. Then search through a brochure to get further details. This will enable you to set up the field names, types and lengths for your database. Below is an example of beach holidays.

Field name	Field type	Field length
Resort		
Holiday no		
Cost		
Departure date		

When you have completed the structure of your database, you can start to enter the information which you have collected. Your database should look like the one given below – though obviously, you will have your own choice of holiday and relevant details.

```
TASK 50

RESORT                HOLIDAY NO        COST        DEPT DATE

Scarborough           AMA65             178         25 July
Bridlington           AMA63             169         14 July
Morecambe             AMA24             155          2 July
Blackpool             AMA21             199         30 July
Colwyn Bay            AMA50             165         14 July
Clacton               AMA40             145          2 July
Brighton              AMA89             180         25 July
Bournemouth           AMA39             200         30 July
Torquay               AMA16             160          2 July
Penzance              AMA77             150          2 July
```

When your database is complete, print it out.

Changing an entry form

In Unit 6 you will practise redesigning and editing an entry form. This will enable you to widen the fields in the database and to add extra fields, if required. You will also look at different ways of entering numbers and text, and will make automatic calculations. In addition, you will save your database as a file on disk so that it can be retrieved for later use. The functions you will look at are:

- Editing an entry form

- Formatting numbers

- Automatic calculations

- Saving and retrieving the database

Editing fields on an entry form

After you have created an entry form, you may realise that it is not suitable for your requirements. You may want to redesign and change its appearance by editing the field names or lengths.

For example, in the hotel database, you may need to extend the field for entering the customer address, as you may not have left enough room for it. You may also want to use abbreviations or shorter field names, as your original choice of field names may have been too long.

```
Record 1
CUSTOMER NAME     _____
CUSTOMER ADDRESS     _____
DATE OF START OF RESERVATION     _____
NUMBER OF NIGHTS  _____
PRICE PER NIGHT  _____
```

Entry form before alteration

Field length altered

```
Record 1
CUSTOMER NAME _____
CUSTOMER ADDRESS _____
BOOKING DATE _____
NO OF NIGHTS _____
TARIFF _____
```

Field names altered

Function	Keystrokes used
Alter field name	....
Alter field length	....
Alter field type	....

Task 51

Design and create an entry form using the information about spending on library books. The field names have been given, but you must decide on the field types and lengths yourself.

Field names
Season
Library
Classification
Acquisitions
Amount spent

Before entering the data, alter the last three field names as shown below. When this has been done, enter the data and print out the whole database.

Category
Number
Sum

Information to be entered in the database

```
TASK 51

LIBRARY            CATEGORY          NUMBER          SUM
SPRING
   Main            Fiction             23            250
   Mobile          Non-fiction          5            100
   Reference       Music                8             90
   Branch          Non-fiction          3             60
SUMMER
   Main            Languages            2             25
   Reference       Computing            3             68
   Branch          Fiction             10             75
AUTUMN
   Main            Biography            2             24
   Reference       Science              6            123
WINTER
   Main            Non-fiction         36            720
   Mobile          Fiction             10             90
   Reference       Encyclopedia         1             50
   Branch          Fiction             20            200
```

Task 52

Design and create an entry form using the information about zoo animals. The field names have been given, but you must decide on the field types and lengths yourself.

When the form has been created, enter the data given below and print out the whole database.

Field names	Abbreviations
Animal	C = carnivorous (meat-eating)
Keeper	H = herbivorous (plant-eating)
Food	I = insectivorous (insect-eating)
Enclosure no	
Location	

Information to be entered in the database

```
TASK 52

ANIMAL          KEEPER          FOOD     ENCLOSURE NO      LOCATION


Lion            Reynolds        C                  8       North
Elephant        Peters          H                 15       Central
Giraffe         Collins         H                 39       South
Camel           Collins         H                 40       South
Crocodile       Shaw            C                 20       East
Monkey          Peters          H                 12       Central
Walrus          Shaw            C                 22       East
Tiger           Reynolds        C                  7       North
Armadillo       Collins         I                 36       South
Llama           Peters          H                 12       Central
```

Complete the alterations below.

Change the field name FOOD to DIET.

Change the field name ENCLOSURE NO to ENC NO and change its field length to 6.

Alter the field length of ANIMAL so that you can enter the following two records.

| Rhinoceros | Shaw | C | 21 | East |
| Hippopotamus | Shaw | C | 23 | East |

Print out the whole database again.

◼ Inserting a field

Sometimes it may be necessary to insert another field in the entry form, so that additional data can be added to the database.

In the zoo database (Task 52), the original entry form looked like this:

```
┌──────────────────────────────────────────────────────────────┐
│ ANIMAL ─────────────────────────                              │
│ KEEPER ───────────────────────                                │
│ FOOD ─────────────────────                                    │
│ ENCLOSURE NO ───────                                          │
│ LOCATION ───────────────                                      │
└──────────────────────────────────────────────────────────────┘
```

Original entry form

If necessary, an extra field, **EXPECTED LIFE SPAN**, could have been inserted.

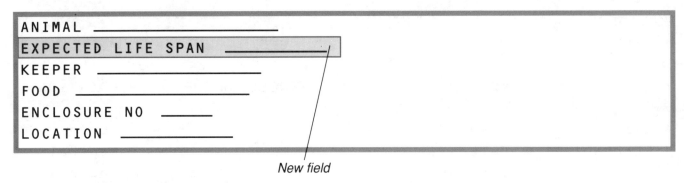

New field

◼ Deleting a field

Similarly, an unnecessary field can be deleted from the entry form, if the information it contains is not useful.

```
┌──────────────────────────────────────────────────────────────┐
│ COUNTRY  ───────────────────────────────                      │
│ CAPITAL  ──────────────────────────                           │
│ MAIN AIRPORT ─────────────────                                │
│ CURRENCY ─────────────────                                    │
│ EXCHANGE RATE ─────────────                                   │
└──────────────────────────────────────────────────────────────┘
```

Unnecessary field

```
┌──────────────────────────────────────────────────────────────┐
│ COUNTRY  ───────────────────────────────                      │
│ CAPITAL  ──────────────────────────                           │
│ CURRENCY ─────────────────────────                            │
│ EXCHANGE RATE ─────────────                                   │
└──────────────────────────────────────────────────────────────┘
```

Amended entry form with field deleted

Function	Keystrokes used
Insert a field	....
Delete a field	....

Task 53

Design and create an entry form using the information about activities at a sports centre this year and next. The field names have been given, but you must decide on the field types and lengths yourself.

When the form has been created, enter the data given below and print out the whole database.

Field names
Centre
Activity
Start
Finish
Course

Information to be entered in the database

```
TASK 53

CENTRE          ACTIVITY        START         FINISH        COURSE

Cranley         Swimming        8 Sept        18 Dec        CR10
Fernhead        Judo           10 Jan         1 July        FR15
Cranley         Football        3 Oct         8 March       CR11
Cranley         Jogging         8 April       29 June       CR19
Bilton          Squash         10 Jan         20 March      BN33
Bilton          Badminton       7 Jan         17 March      BN34
Cranley         Golf            2 May         30 June       CR26
Cranley         Tennis          6 April       27 June       CR23
Fernhead        Aikido         12 Jan         20 March      FR17
Fernhead        Yoga           14 Sept        25 June       FR14
```

Amend the database so that a new field COST is inserted between ACTIVITY and START. Add the entries shown below to the records. Print out the entire database again.

COST 24   45   43   20   28   28   37   33   21   57

Design and create an entry form using the information about yearly hospital casualty ward complaints. The field names have been given, but you must decide on the field types and lengths yourself.

When the form has been created, enter the data given below and print out the whole database.

Field names
Hospital
Patient
Complaint
Referred (by GPs)
No of visits

Information to be entered in the database

```
TASK 54

HOSPITAL            PATIENT         COMPLAINT       REFERRED    VISITS

St Lukes            Briggs S        Cuts            Yes            2
Manor Park          Walker B        Dog bite        Yes            5
Parkside            Milton R        Flu             No             1
The Chase           Walmsley P      Pneumonia       Yes           10
Manor Park          Smith C         Burns           Yes           20
Parkside            Harris F        Eye injury      No             7
Royal Infirmary     Stavros S       Sprain          No             4
St Lukes            Hawton A        Fracture        No            10
Royal Infirmary     Carter L        Burns           Yes            9
The Chase           Barrows J       Fracture        No            11
```

Amend the database so that the field **REFERRED** is deleted. Make sure that all the entries that have been made in this field in the records are also deleted.

Entering numbers

It is wise to keep fields as narrow as possible, so that you can view the whole width of your database and print it on a sheet of A4 paper.

Large numbers often present a problem. If a number is entered as

63,290,000

it will take up ten spaces, because of the commas between the digits. It is better to enter it as

63290000

because this is shorter and only takes up eight spaces. Better still would be to indicate in the field name that the number is in thousands, so that it can be entered without the last three zeros, like this:

```
000s  ────────────── Field name
63290 ────────────── Record entry
```

Sums of money can be entered using a 'pounds and pence' format which shows two decimal places. For example, forty-eight pounds will be displayed as

48.00

Using abbreviations

You must also use abbreviations wherever possible to keep the field lengths in your database as short as you can. This will give the database a neater design, and allow you to enter more fields, if required.

```
LANGUAGE            AREAS WHERE SPOKEN          NUMBER OF SPEAKERS
Arabic              Middle East, North Africa        187,000,000
Mandarin Chinese    North China, East China          825,000,000
Portuguese          Portugal, Brazil                 169,000,000
Spanish             Spain, South America             320,000,000
```

A poorly designed database with long fields and numbers

M = millions

```
LANGUAGE      WHERE SPOKEN            NO (M)
Arabic        Middle East, N Africa     187
Mandarin      N China, E China          825
Portuguese    Portugal, Brazil          169
Spanish       Spain, S America          320
```

A better design with room for extra fields

In the remaining tasks, you will be expected to format numbers so that they take up as little space as possible, and to use sensible abbreviations wherever possible. You should use your own judgement in these matters.

Design and create an entry form using the information about the planets in the solar system. Though the field names have been given, you must abbreviate them and format the numbers where possible. You must also decide on the field types and lengths yourself.

When the form has been created, enter the data given below, and print out the whole database.

Field names
Name of planet
Distance from sun in km
Diameter in km
Number of satellites

Information to be entered in the database

```
TASK 55

PLANET        DISTANCE IN KM      DIAMETER IN KM      NO OF SATELLITES

Mercury           58,000,000               4,878                     0
Venus            108,000,000              12,104                     0
Earth            150,000,000              12,756                     1
Mars             228,000,000               6,794                     2
Jupiter          778,000,000             142,800                    16
Saturn         1,427,000,000             120,000                    21
Uranus         2,870,000,000              52,000                    15
Neptune        4,497,000,000              48,400                     2
Pluto          5,900,000,000               3,000                     1
```

Task 56

Design and create an entry form using the information about the world's most highly populated cities. Though the field names have been given, you must abbreviate them and format the numbers where possible. You must also decide on the field types and lengths yourself.

When the form has been created, enter the data given below and print out the whole database.

Field names
Name of continent
Name of country
Name of city
Total population

Information to be entered in the database

```
TASK 56

COUNTRY                CITY              POPULATION


ASIA
Japan                  Tokyo             25,434,000
South Korea            Seoul             13,665,000
India                  Calcutta          10,462,000
China                  Shanghai          12,620,000


NORTH AMERICA
USA                    New York          14,598,000
USA                    Los Angeles        3,260,000


SOUTH AMERICA
Mexico                 Mexico City       16,901,000
Brazil                 Sao Paulo         14,911,000
Argentina              Buenos Aires      10,750,000


EUROPE
USSR                   Moscow             8,815,000
France                 Paris              8,707,000
Britain                London             6,775,000
```

Automatic calculations

Sometimes you may not want a database simply for storing information. You may want it to complete a calculation as well. This will always be the case if you have specified one of the field types on the entry form as a **calculation field**. A calculation field works out the value that is to appear in the database.

For example, if the database holds information about customer purchases, you will want the QUANTITY field multiplied by the UNIT PRICE field to give you the value for the TOTAL £ field. By defining this as an automatic calculation, the value will automatically be entered in the TOTAL £ field in the database.

```
Record 1
CUSTOMER NAME      Johnson Ltd
ITEM       Tennis racket
QUANTITY       100
UNIT PRICE       75.00
TOTAL £
```

This field is automatically calculated

CUSTOMER NAME	ITEM	QUANTITY	UNIT PRICE	TOTAL £
Johnson Ltd	Tennis racket	100	75.00	7500.00
Supersport	Cricket bat	100	50.00	5000.00
Win-well Ltd	Football	100	25.00	2500.00

Calculations from each record will be entered in the database

Saving and retrieving the database

When you use a database management system, the information you enter appears on the screen while the computer is switched on, but it will be lost when the computer is switched off, unless you save it on a disk.

You must save your work as a file on a disk if you want to keep a permanent record of it. Each file must have its own special name so that you can retrieve it without difficulty.

Every time you want to work on the file, you must retrieve it from disk. Any fresh work that you do on the database must be saved again on disk, or the changes you made will be lost.

In the next set of tasks, you will be expected to save your work on disk and retrieve it.

Function	Keystrokes used
Perform an automatic calculation	....
Save on disk	....
Retrieve from disk	....

Task 57

Design and create an entry form using the information about customer orders. Though the field names have been given, you must decide on the field types and lengths yourself. You are also expected to complete the calculation field by means of an automatic calculation.

When the form has been created, enter the data given below, and print out the whole database.

Field names
Customer
Item
Quantity
Price
Total

Information to be entered in the database

```
TASK 57

CUSTOMER          ITEM             QUANTITY     PRICE    TOTAL

Grow-Fast Ltd     Digging fork        100       12.99
Milton Tools      Border spade         50       11.99
Jacksons          Garden rake          25        8.49
The Garden Shop   Trowel               60        3.50
Goodmans Ltd      Hand shears          75        9.99
Lawn Centre       Lawn shears         120       10.00
Freshfields       Secateurs           100        5.49
Garden Care Co    Digging spade        30       12.99
Le Jardin         Compost bin          10       24.00
Essex Gardens     Wheelbarrow           5       18.00
```

Design and create an entry form using the information about women prime ministers and presidents. Though the field names have been given, you must decide on the field types and lengths yourself.

When the form has been created, enter the data given below, print out the whole database, and save it on disk.

Field names	Abbreviations
Status	PM = Prime Minister
Surname	PR = President
Country	
Elected	

Information to be entered in the database

```
TASK 58

SURNAME                 COUNTRY              ELECTED


PRIME MINISTER
Bandaranaike            Ceylon               1960
Gandhi                  India                1966
Meir                    Israel               1969
Domitien                Central Africa       1975
Thatcher                UK                   1979
Pintasilgo              Portugal             1979
Charles                 Dominica             1980
Brundtland              Norway               1981


PRESIDENT
Peron                   Argentina            1974
Finnbogadottir          Iceland              1980
```

Retrieve Task 58 from disk, and make the following amendments. Insert a new field, **FIRST NAME**, between **SURNAME** and **COUNTRY**, with the information shown below, and add four new records to the database. When it is complete, print it out.

TASK 58

STATUS	SURNAME		COUNTRY	ELECTED	FIRST NAME
PM	Bandaranaike		Ceylon	1960	Sirimavo
PM	Gandhi		India	1966	Indira
PM	Meir		Israel	1969	Golda
PM	Domitien		Central Africa	1975	Elisabeth
PM	Thatcher		UK	1979	Margaret
PM	Pintasilgo		Portugal	1979	Maria
PM	Charles		Dominica	1980	Eugenia
PM	Brundtland		Norway	1981	Gro
PR	Peron		Argentina	1974	Maria
PR	Finnbogadottir		Iceland	1980	Vigdis
PR	Aquino	Corazon	Philippines	1986	
PM	Bhutto	Benazir	Pakistan	1988	
PR	Chamorro	Violetta	Nicaragua	1990	
PR	Pascal-Trouillot	Ertha	Haiti	1990	
PM	Zia	Khaleda	Bangladesh	1991	

Task 59

(1) Load your database program.

(2) Refer to the data to be used and create a database containing the following fields, using suitable abbreviations where necessary.

Field names	Abbreviations
Office	HO = Head Office
Name	LO = Liverpool Office
Job	WO = Widnes Office
Date of birth	DOB = Date of birth
Years service	YS = Years service

(3) Enter the following details:

```
NAME                    JOB                DOB            YS

HEAD OFFICE
Lundy K                 WP Operator        8/3/50          5
Patterson J             Clerk              12/2/55         3
Welch F                 Secretary          21/6/47         9
Vyos R                  Receptionist       31/1/70         6

LIVERPOOL OFFICE
Albany S                WP Operator        6/9/65          4
Sanders R               Clerk              14/11/61        8
Thursby A               Clerk              2/5/69          3

WIDNES OFFICE
Garrick H               Bookkeeper         22/7/70         1
King M                  Secretary          18/10/56        7
Phillips T              Clerk              30/3/54         8
```

(4) Save and print your database.

(5) Recall the database and delete the field **YEARS SERVICE**, amending all the records.

(6) The following details need to be amended:

Thursby is a secretary, not a clerk.

Lundy's date of birth is 28/3/60, not 8/3/50.

King's initial is A, not M, and she works in the Liverpool Office, not the Widnes Office.

(7) Save and print the database again.

Task 60 – home-buying database

For Task 60, set up a database which provides information about properties for sale in the area. For this task you will need a local newspaper which has a selection of houses and flats for sale.

When you have studied the newspaper, decide what price range you are going to look at, then plan out the field names, types and lengths for your database. Below is a suggestion, but you can use your own fields.

Field name	Field type	Field length
Estate agent		
Area		
Type of accommodation		
No of bedrooms		
Price		

When you have completed the structure of your database, enter the information which you have collected. Below is a short example based on the field names already given.

```
TASK 60

AGENT            AREA            TYPE          NO OF BEDS    PRICE £

Denmans          Northwood       Terraced            2      80,000
Conelly          Grange Park     Semi                3      95,000
Wilton & Co      Northwood       Semi                3      86,000
Denmans          Grange Park     Terraced            3      82,000
```

When your database is complete, print it out.

Then go back and practise making alterations to your database. Change one of the items in the database and look through the newspaper again to see if you can make suitable alterations.

For example, increase the price range you are looking at by £10,000 and see if there are any houses in the same areas for the new sum of money. If so, alter the details accordingly.

Another possible alteration would be to look at different areas and see if there are houses of a similar price in the new areas.

When you have finished making the alterations, print out the new database.

Sorting records

Records are inserted in the database in the same order that they are entered on the entry form. As this may not always be convenient, it is possible to sort the records into a different order. In this unit you will learn about sorting records in different ways:

- Sorting alphabetically
- Sorting numerically
- Sorting chronologically (in date order)
- Erasing the database

Sorting records alphabetically

The records in the database below have not been sorted, and they appear in the same order in which they were entered on the entry form. New records will always be displayed at the bottom of the database. The records can be sorted alphabetically in either ascending order or decending order.

PATIENT'S NAME	NHS NUMBER	DATE OF BIRTH
Simmons R A	100539	12-Oct-70
Atkins C J	600356	27-Mar-69
Zinkin P M	800365	30-Nov-71
Matthews D L	200928	05-Jan-65

Records appear in the order they have been entered

When records are sorted in **ascending order**, they will be arranged alphabetically from A to Z.

PATIENT'S NAME	NHS NUMBER	DATE OF BIRTH
Atkins C J	600356	27-Mar-69
Matthews D L	200928	05-Jan-65
Simmons R A	100539	12-Oct-70
Zinkin P M	800365	30-Nov-71

Records in ascending alphabetical order

When records are sorted in **descending order**, they will be arranged alphabetically from Z to A.

PATIENT'S NAME	NHS NUMBER	DATE OF BIRTH
Zinkin P M	800365	30-Nov-71
Simmons R A	100539	12-Oct-70
Matthews D L	200928	05-Jan-65
Atkins C J	600356	27-Mar-69

Records in descending alphabetical order

Function	Keystrokes used
Define field to be sorted	....
Sort alphabetically in ascending order	....
Sort alphabetically in descending order	....

Task 61

Design and create an entry form using the information about permit holders for a company's car-parks. The field names have been given, but you must decide on the field types and lengths yourself.

When you have entered the data, sort it alphabetically in ascending order of permit holder's name and print out the entire database. Then re-sort in descending order and print it out again.

Field names	Abbreviations
Car-park	
Permit holder's name	NAME
Car	
Colour	
Registration number	REG NO

Information to be entered in the database

```
TASK 61


NAME                    CAR             COLOUR          REG NO


MAIN PARK
Harrington P            Nissan          Red             E346 LHV
Gupta A                 Vauxhall        White           F415 ELU
Mackenzie A             Ford            White           D300 FLK
Chapman M               Citroen         Green           H214 KHL
Wrightson J             Renault         Blue            H468 JLR
Edwards P               Volvo           Black           G613 HMN


OVERFLOW PARK
Garbutt D               Toyota          Grey            G941 FTM
Bridgewater T           Nissan          Red             D588 KLM
Livingstone M           Honda           White           G820 SLX
Johnstone R             Vauxhall        Black           H912 JKR
```

Task 62

Design and create an entry form using the information about local restaurants. The field names have been given, but you must decide on the field types and lengths yourself.

When you have entered the data, sort it alphabetically in ascending order of restaurant name, and print out the entire database. Then re-sort in descending order and print it out again.

Field names	Abbreviations
Location	
Restaurant name	
Type	
Map reference	REF
Number of days open per week	DAYS OPEN

Information to be entered in the database

```
TASK 62

RESTAURANT NAME        TYPE           REF        DAYS OPEN

TOWN CENTRE
Ye Olde White Lion     English        D7              7
Captain's Table        English        E4              7
Trattoria              Italian        E9              6
Jade Lantern           Chinese        C5              6
Rajput                 Indian         D4              7
Singapore Inn          Malaysian      C3              5
Olive Grove            Greek          E3              6

OUT-OF-TOWN
Cafe de Paris          French         K12             5
All Seasons Inn        English        L14             5
Mont Saint Michel      French         J10             6
```

Task 63

(1) Load your database program.

(2) Refer to the data given below and create an entry form containing the following fields, using abbreviations where necessary:

Field names
Variety
Name
Time
Plants attacked
Site of damage

(3) Enter the following details:

NAME	TIME	PLANTS ATTACKED	SITE OF DAMAGE
SOIL PESTS			
Slugs	Night	Lettuce	Leaves
Wireworms	All year	Crops	Roots
Leather-jackets	Spring	Young plants	Roots
LEAF-EATING PESTS			
Winter moth	Spring	Flowers	Flowers
Caterpillars	Summer	Cabbage	Leaves
Pea thrip	Summer	Peas	Pods
SUCKING PESTS			
Green fly	Summer	Roses	Flowers
Ants	All year	Lawns	Surface
Red spider	Dry spells	Plants	Leaves
Gall weevil	Spring	Turnips	Roots

(4) Sort the records alphabetically in ascending order (i.e. from A to Z) using the NAME field.

(5) Save the database and print out a copy.

(6) Add the following record under SOIL PESTS:

    Millepedes   All year   Vegetables   Roots

(7) Add the following record under LEAF-EATING PESTS:

    Apple sawfly   Summer   Apples   Fruit

(8) Alter the record for Ants. They attack lawns in summer only, not all year round.

(9) Sort the records into ascending alphabetical order again.

(10) Print out the entire database.

Sorting records numerically

Records that contain a number field can be sorted numerically. If the number field consists of sums of money, then these too will be arranged numerically. Ascending or descending order can be used.

When records are sorted in *ascending order*, they will be arranged with the smallest number first and the largest number last.

PATIENT'S NAME	NHS NUMBER	DATE OF BIRTH
Simmons R A	100539	12-Oct-70
Matthews D L	200928	05-Jan-65
Atkins C J	600356	27-Mar-69
Zinkin P M	800365	30-Nov-71

Ascending numerical order (smallest number first)

When records are sorted in *descending order*, they will be arranged with the largest number first and the smallest number last.

PATIENT'S NAME	NHS NUMBER	DATE OF BIRTH
Zinkin P M	800365	30-Nov-71
Atkins C J	600356	27-Mar-69
Matthews D L	200928	05-Jan-65
Simmons R A	100539	12-Oct-70

Descending numerical order (largest number first)

Sorting sums of money

Records that have a number field containing a sum of money can be sorted in exactly the same way.

DESTINATION	TICKET TYPE	COST IN £
Los Angeles	Return	299.95
Hong Kong	Return	479.00
Tokyo	Return	588.50
Sydney	Return	790.99

Air fares sorted into ascending numerical order

DESTINATION	TICKET TYPE	COST IN £
Sydney	Return	790.99
Tokyo	Return	588.50
Hong Kong	Return	479.00
Los Angeles	Return	299.95

Air fares sorted into descending numerical order

Function	Keystrokes used
Define field to be sorted	....
Sort numerically in ascending order	....
Sort numerically in descending order	....

Task 64

Design and create an entry form using the information about students' exam results. The field names have been given, but you must decide on the field types and lengths yourself.

When you have entered the data, sort the exam marks numerically in ascending order and print out the entire database. Then re-sort in descending order and print it out again.

Field names	**Abbreviations**
Subject	ACC = Accountancy
Surname	CP = Computer programming
First name	ECON = Economics
Faculty	
Result	
Mark	

Information to be entered in the database

```
TASK 64

SURNAME                    FIRST NAME   FACULTY     RESULT      MARK

ACCOUNTANCY
Crosby                     Paul         Business    Pass        54
Fitzhugh                   Angela       Business    Pass        69
Greaves                    Julie        Business    Fail        38

COMPUTER PROGRAMMING
Hadley                     Rosemary     Science     Credit      70
Ashcroft                   Daniel       Science     Credit      73
Orpington                  Alan         Science     Pass        62

ECONOMICS
Goodman                    Simon        Maths       Referred    47
Nomikos                    Elena        Maths       Pass        64

LAW
Jackson                    Roger        Business    Pass        57
Upland                     Michelle     Business    Pass        56
```

Task 65

Design and create an entry form using the information about day trips by coach. The field names have been given, but you must decide on the field types and lengths yourself.

When you have entered the data, sort the prices numerically in ascending order and print out the entire database. Then re-sort in descending order and print it out again.

Field names	Abbreviations
Departure point	DP = Departure point
Destination	V = Victoria
Location	RS = Russell Square
Travel time	TIME = Travel time
Cost £	

Information to be entered in the database

```
TASK 65

DESTINATION            LOCATION          TIME           COST £


VICTORIA
Roman Baths            Bath              3h             11.25
Royal Pavilion         Brighton          1h 45m          7.25
Leeds Castle           Kent              1h 30m         10.00
Stonehenge             Wilts             2h 40m         10.50
The Cathedral          Canterbury        2h 50m          7.55
State Apartments       Windsor           1h              8.50


RUSSELL SQUARE
Alton Towers           Staffs            3h 40m         19.00
The University         Cambridge         2h              7.75
Viking Centre          York              4h 20m         20.00
Illuminations          Blackpool         5h             25.00
```

Sorting records chronologically (in date order)

By now you will be aware that a date field in a record always has three elements: the day, the month and the year. When records are sorted chronologically, the year of the date will always be sorted first, followed by the month, and then the day.

When records are sorted in *ascending order*, they will be arranged with the earliest date first and the latest date last.

PATIENT'S NAME	NHS NUMBER	DATE OF BIRTH
Matthews D L	200928	05-Jan-65
Atkins C J	600356	27-Mar-69
Simmons R A	100539	12-Oct-70
Zinkin P M	800365	30-Nov-71

Ascending chronological order (earliest year first)

When records are sorted in *descending order*, they will be arranged with the latest date first and the earliest date last.

PATIENT'S NAME	NHS NUMBER	DATE OF BIRTH
Zinkin P M	800365	30-Nov-71
Simmons R A	100539	12-Oct-70
Atkins C J	600356	27-Mar-69
Matthews D L	200928	05-Jan-65

Descending chronological order (latest year first)

Sorting in month order

Sometimes, only one year may be involved in a date field. If this is the case, the dates will be sorted in order of month. When *ascending order* is used, the months are sorted from January to December.

NATIONAL EXHIBITION CENTRE	DATE
Holiday Show	16-Jan-92
Computers For All Exhibition	08-Mar-92
Personal Finance Fair	02-Oct-92

Ascending chronological order (earliest month first)

When *descending order* is used, the months are sorted from December to January.

NATIONAL EXHIBITION CENTRE	DATE
Personal Finance Fair	02-Oct-92
Computers For All Exhibition	08-Mar-92
Holiday Show	16-Jan-92

Descending chronological order (latest month first)

Function	Keystrokes used
Define field to be sorted	....
Sort chronologically in ascending order	....
Sort chronologically in descending order	....

Task 66

Design and create an entry form using the information about animals treated by a vet. The field names have been given, but you must decide on the field types and lengths yourself.

When you have entered the data, sort the registration dates in ascending order and print out the entire database. Then re-sort in descending order and print it out again.

Field names	Abbreviation
Pet	
Breed	
Name	
Registration date	REG DATE
Owner	

Information to be entered in the database

```
TASK 66

BREED              NAME           REG DATE        OWNER

DOG
Alsatian           Prince         2/9/83          Smith E
Labrador           Jamie          19/3/84         Winrow K
Bull Terrier       Bella          29/6/91         McIntyre R
Poodle             Gemma          30/9/86         Waddington P
Dachshund          Meg            7/12/90         Fisher H
Mongrol            Toby           17/8/87         Richardson J

CAT
Persian            Sasha          16/9/88         Boardwick G
Siamese            Bijou          3/1/92          Miller C
Persian            Holly          31/3/85         Baker K
Abyssinian         Hamlet         22/5/89         Derwent A
```

Task 67

Design and create an entry form using the information about magazine subscriptions. The field names have been given, but you must decide on the field types and lengths yourself.

When you have entered the data, sort the renewal dates in ascending order and print out the entire database. Then re-sort in descending order and print it out again.

Field names	Abbreviations
Category	
Magazine	
Subscriber	
Subscriber number	NO
Renewal date	REN DATE

Information to be entered in the database

```
TASK 67

MAGAZINE                    SUBSCRIBER        NO       REN DATE


COMPUTERS
Your Home Computer          Jackson M         692      2/6/92
Pick a PC                   Wilks I           849      18/9/92
Software News               Littleton W       349      12/8/92
Bits and Bytes              Collingtree A     265      27/4/92


SPORT
Sportspeople                Lacey T           483      8/3/92
Personal Fitness            Billingham R      368      12/1/92
Country Walking             Hawton J          226      31/3/92
The World of Tennis         Wilmington E      797      27/11/92
Sports Outlook              Winkworth S       904      5/1/92


FINANCE
Good Investment Guide       Turner D          941      20/10/92
Spending and Saving         Smythe R          435      22/12/92
Personal Finances           Dickinson A       650      4/4/92
```

Erasing a database

A database created by you can be erased from screen if you have no more use for it. The database management system, which is the computer program that allows you to make your own database, will not be affected by this.

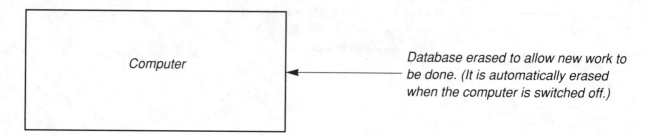

Database erased to allow new work to be done. (It is automatically erased when the computer is switched off.)

Erasing a database from disk

A database can be saved as a file on disk and retrieved later for use. If new work is done on the database, it must be saved again on disk and the original file must be overwritten. If the file is not required any more, it can be erased from disk.

Saving and retrieving

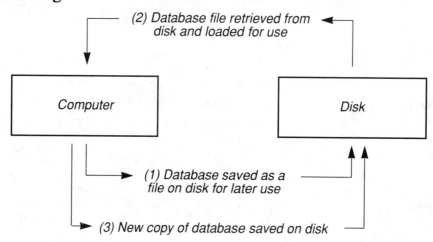

(2) Database file retrieved from disk and loaded for use

(1) Database saved as a file on disk for later use

(3) New copy of database saved on disk

Saving and erasing

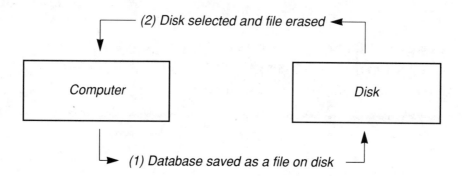

(2) Disk selected and file erased

(1) Database saved as a file on disk

Function	Keystrokes used
Erase database from disk	....

Task 68

Design and create an entry form using the information about worldwide industrial accidents in recent years. The field names have been given, but you must decide on the field types and lengths yourself.

When you have entered the data, sort the field for lives lost in ascending order (the highest number last) and print out the entire database. Then re-sort in descending order (the highest number first), save as a file on disk and print it out again.

Field names
Year
Location
Cause
Lives lost

Information to be entered in the database

TASK 68

YEAR	LOCATION	CAUSE	LIVES LOST
1970	Osaka	Gas explosion	92
1978	Los Alfaques	Oil explosion	216
1978	Hulmanguille	Gas explosion	58
1979	Novosibirsk	Chemical accident	300
1980	Otvella	Explosives accident	51
1980	Bangkok	Armament explosion	54
1981	Tacoa	Oil explosion	145
1983	Sao Paulo	Gas explosion	508
1984	Bhopal	Chemical leakage	2500
1986	Chernobyl	Nuclear explosion	29

Retrieve Task 68 from disk and make the following amendments. Insert a new field COUNTRY between LOCATION and CAUSE, with the information shown below.

Add three new records to the database and make the alterations shown.

Re-sort the database in ascending numerical order using the YEAR field, and print it out. Erase the file from disk.

TASK 68

YEAR	LOCATION	CAUSE	LIVES LOST	COUNTRY
1970	Osaka	Gas explosion	92	Japan
1978	Los Alfaques	Oil explosion	216	Spain
1978	Hulmanguille	Gas explosion	58	Mexico
1979	Novosibirsk	Chemical accident	300	USSR
1980	Otvella	Explosives accident	51	Spain
1980	Bangkok	Armament explosion	54	Thailand
1981	Tacoa	Oil explosion	145	Venezuela
1984 ~~1983~~	Sao Paulo	Gas explosion	508	Brazil
1984	Bhopal	Chemical leakage	2500	India
1986	Chernobyl	Nuclear explosion	29	USSR
1984	Gahri Dhoda	Pakistan	Gas explosion	60
1982	Caracas	Venezuela	Explosives accident	101
1978	Xilatopec	Mexico	Gas explosion	100

Task 69

(1) Load your database program.

(2) Refer to the data given below and create an entry form containing the following fields:

Field names
Fruit
Name
Variety
Growth
Use

(3) Enter the following details:

NAME	VARIETY	GROWTH	READY FOR USE
APPLE			
Lord Derby	Cooking	Upright	Sept-Mar
Blenheim Orange	Cooking	Spreading	Nov-Jan
Cox's Orange Pippin	Dessert	Spreading	Nov-Mar
Bramley's Seedling	Cooking	Spreading	Sept-Mar
Worcester Pearmain	Dessert	Upright	Sept-Oct
James Grieve	Dessert	Upright	Sept-Oct
Ribston Pippin	Dessert	Spreading	Dec
PEAR			
Conference	Dessert	Upright	Nov-Dec
Catillac	Cooking	Spreading	Sept
Laxton's Superb	Dessert	Spreading	Aug
Fertility	Cooking	Upright	Sept
Doyenne Du Comice	Dessert	Spreading	Oct-Nov

(4) Sort the records alphabetically in ascending order (i.e. from A to Z) using the **NAME** field. Save the database as a file on disk and print out a copy.

(5) Delete the record for Ribston Pippin, and add the following record under **APPLE:**
    Fearn's Pippin   Dessert   Upright   Dec-Mar

(6) Add the following record under **PEAR:**
    Winter Nelis   Dessert   Spreading   Nov-Feb

(7) Alter the record for Blenheim Orange. This is a dessert apple, not a cooking apple.

(8) Alter the record for Conference pears. These grow on a spreading tree, not an upright one.

(9) Sort the records into ascending alphabetical order again.

(10) Print out the entire database, then erase the file from disk.

Task 70

(1) Load your database program.

(2) Refer to the data given below and create an entry form containing the following fields:

Field names	Abbreviations
Type	
Name of desert	DESERT
Location	
Inhabitants	
Area in sq km	SQ KM 000S

(3) Enter the following details:

DESERT	LOCATION	INHABITANTS	SQ KM 000S
SAND			
Sahara	North Africa	Berbers	9000
Arabian	SW Asia	Bedouin	1300
Takla Mahan	China	Chinese	327
Sonoran	Mexico	Mexicans	310
SCRUB			
Australian	Australia	Aborigines	3830
Kalahari	Botswana	Hottentots	520
Namib	Namibia	Bushmen	310
Somali	Somalia	Somalis	260
STEPPE			
Gobi	Mongolia	Nomads	1295
Turkestan	Central Asia	Uzbeks	450

(4) Sort your database numerically in ascending order (i.e. from the smallest number to the largest) using the SQ KM field. Save it as a file on disk and print out a copy.

(5) Delete the record for the Australian desert, and add the following records under SCRUB:

Tamami	Australia	Aborigines	957
Gibson	Australia	Aborigines	959
Gt Victoria	Australia	Aborigines	957

(6) Add the following record under SAND:

Great Sandy   Australia   Aborigines   957

(7) Alter the inhabitants of Turkestan to Nomads.

(8) Sort the database into descending numerical order (largest number first).

(9) Print out the entire database, then erase the file from disk.

You will probably need a national newspaper for Task 71, as you are going to set up a database of long-distance flights and the cost of a one-way and a return ticket.

First pick at least three different continents and several different destinations in these continents. You can then divide up the destinations into the towns and the countries in which they are located. Then plan out the field names, types and lengths. Below is an example to help you.

Field names	Abbreviations
Continent	SA = South America
Destination	OW = One way
Country	RTN = Return
One way	
Return	

When you have planned out the structure of the database, enter the information you have collected. Study the example given, but do not copy it.
When your database is complete, save it on disk and print it out.

DESTINATION	COUNTRY	OW	RTN
SOUTH AMERICA			
Rio de Janeiro	Brazil	315	510
Buenos Aires	Argentina	410	645
Bogota	Colombia	259	400
Caracas	Venezuela	255	420
ASIA			
Bangkok	Thailand	220	375
Jakarta	Indonesia	240	460
Singapore	Malaysia	210	410
Peking	China	265	520
AFRICA			
Nairobi	Kenya	255	395
Lusaka	Zambia	285	540
Lagos	Nigeria	209	389
Harare	Zimbabwe	259	449

Recall the database, sort it into alphabetical order of destination and print it out again.

Lastly, recall the database again, sort it into descending numerical order of return fares (from the highest to the lowest), and print it out again.

Selecting records

Unit 8 concentrates on using a partial database. It will enable you to make a selection of the records you want to deal with, and print them out. This selection can be further refined, if required, and a limited number of fields can be chosen for the final print out. The areas you will focus on are:

- Selecting records

- Printing a selection of records

- Narrowing the selection

- Printing a partial database

Selecting records

Sometimes, you may not want to deal with the whole of your database, but may want to use only certain records, and print them out.

It is possible to do this, providing you define exactly which records you are interested in. For example, a company may need to contact only certain of its employees – say, its computer operators – and it may be helpful to have a printed list of their names and the departments they work in.

In this case, it will be necessary for the database to be searched until all the records of staff who fulfil the job specification of computer operator are found. As a result, you will be provided with only a selection of records.

NAME	JOB	DEPARTMENT
Atkins Annette	Sales clerk	Marketing
Harris Desmond	Computer operator	Personnel
Langley Sharon	Accounts clerk	Finance
Pearce Marie	Computer operator	Purchasing
Rawlings Ian	Computer operator	Personnel

Staff list before selection

NAME	JOB	DEPARTMENT
Harris Desmond	Computer operator	Personnel
Pearce Marie	Computer operator	Purchasing
Rawlings Ian	Computer operator	Personnel

Staff list after selection of computer operators

You can continue work with this limited list of records, and it can be printed out if required.

Function	Keystrokes used
Define selection of records	....
Print out selection of records	....

Task 72

Design and create an entry form using the information about local bus services. The field names have been given, but you must decide on the field types and lengths yourself.

When you have entered the data, print out the entire database. Then select only those records for double-decker buses and print them out.

Field names	Abbreviations
Starting point	BS = Bus station
Route no	SC = Shopping centre
Type	BG = Bus garage
Fare stages	
Operation	

Information to be entered in the database

```
TASK 72


ROUTE NO          TYPE              FARE STAGES   OPERATION


BUS STATION
221               Double-decker         24        Driver-operated
360               Single-decker         20        Driver-operated
366               Double-decker         30        Conductor
H3                Mini-bus              12        Flat fare


SHOPPING CENTRE
190               Double-decker         30        Conductor
113               Single-decker         20        Driver-operated
176               Double-decker         24        Conductor


BUS GARAGE
Tourist           Open-top               0        Flat fare
Dial-a-bus        Mini-bus              20        Flat fare
259               Double-decker         30        Conductor
```

Design and create an entry form using the information about crime statistics. The field names have been given, but you must decide on the field types and lengths yourself.

When you have entered the data, print out the entire database. Then select only those records for burglaries and print them out.

Field names	Abbreviations
Month	SEPT = September
Crime	OCT = October
Time of day	NOV = November
Location	TIME = Time of day
How reported	

Information to be entered in the database

```
TASK 73


CRIME              TIME            LOCATION              HOW REPORTED


SEPTEMBER
Robbery            Morning         Building society      Phone
Burglary           Evening         Private house         In person
Assault            Night           In the street         In person
Armed attack       Afternoon       Bank                  By a witness


OCTOBER
Burglary           Afternoon       Private house         Phone
Assault            Evening         On the tube           Traffic police
Manslaughter       Night           In the street         By a passer-by


NOVEMBER
Burglary           Evening         Private house         In person
Burglary           Afternoon       Art gallery           Phone
Arson              Night           Warehouse             Phone
Robbery            Mid-day         Building society      Phone
Child kidnap       Morning         School playground     By witnesses
```

Task 74

(1) Load your database program.

(2) Refer to the data given below and create an entry form containing the following fields, using abbreviations where necessary:

Field names
Type
Name
Use
Flavour
Remarks

(3) Enter the following details:

NAME	USE	FLAVOUR	REMARKS
HERB			
Sage	Culinary	Aromatic	Popular in stuffing
Aconite	Medicinal	Strong	Poisonous root
Rosemary	Culinary	Sweetish	Common with lamb
Mint	Culinary	Distinctive	Best fresh
Lavendar	Perfume	Sweet	Produces oil
Wormwood	Medicinal	Bitter	Bitter plant
Chamomile	Medicinal	Mild	Used as tea
Thyme	Culinary	Pungent	Popular in stuffing
Horehound	Medicinal	Bitter	Juice used
SPICE			
Paprika	Culinary	Mild and sweet	Used as a garnish
Caraway	Culinary	Warm	Seeds also used
Chillies	Culinary	Very hot	Use warily

(4) Sort the records alphabetically in ascending order (i.e. from A to Z) using the NAME field.

(5) Print out a copy of the entire database.

(6) Delete the details for caraway from the database, as, unlike the other herbs and spices, it cannot be grown in Britain.

(7) Select those herbs and spices that have only a culinary use.

(8) Print out the selected records.

Narrowing the selection

Records can be selected from a database using more than one field for the selection. Using the example at the start of this unit, it is possible to select not only those staff who work as computer operators, but those who work as *computer operators* in the *Personnel Department*.

NAME	JOB	DEPARTMENT
Atkins Annette	Sales clerk	Marketing
Harris Desmond	Computer operator	Personnel
Langley Sharon	Accounts clerk	Finance
Pearce Marie	Computer operator	Purchasing
Rawlings Ian	Computer operator	Personnel

Staff list before selection

NAME	JOB	DEPARTMENT
Harris Desmond	Computer operator	Personnel
Pearce Marie	Computer operator	Purchasing
Rawlings Ian	Computer operator	Personnel

Selection made using one field

NAME	JOB	DEPARTMENT
Harris Desmond	Computer operator	Personnel
Rawlings Ian	Computer operator	Personnel

Selection made using two fields

Using numbers in the selection

If the selection of records involves numbers, it is not necessary to choose an exact number. The selection can be based on numbers that are more than or less than a chosen figure.

NAME	COURSE	AGE
Jackson Steven	Computer Literacy	18
Walsingham Mary	BTEC	17
Foster Rachel	Computer Literacy	19
Burton Daniel	Computer Literacy	17

Students before selection

NAME	COURSE	AGE
Jackson Steven	Computer Literacy	18
Foster Rachel	Computer Literacy	19

Selection of Computer Literacy students who are more than 17

Function	Keystrokes used
Define second selection of records	....
Print making two selections	....

Task 75

Design and create an entry form using the information about properties for sale. The field names have been given, but you must decide on the field types and lengths yourself.

When you have entered the data, print out the entire database. Then, select only those records for semi-detached houses and print them out. Search again for all records of semi-detached houses with garages and print them out.

Field names	Abbreviations
Bedrooms	CH = Central heating
Type	SH = Storage heating
Garage	OSP = Off street parking
Heating	
Garden	

Information to be entered in the database

```
TASK 75


TYPE            GARAGE              HEATING             GARDEN


2-BEDROOMED
Terraced        No garage           Storage heating     50 ft
Semi-detached   Garage              Gas CH              20 ft
End of terrace  Garage              None                30 ft
Terraced        Off street parking  Gas CH              15 ft


3-BEDROOMED
Semi-detached   Garage              Gas CH              30 ft
Terraced        No garage           Storage heating     50 ft
Detached        Garage              Gas CH              30 ft
Semi-detached   Garage              Hot air CH          50 ft
Semi-detached   Off street parking  Gas CH              20 ft
Semi-detached   Garage              None                100 ft
```

Task 76

Design and create an entry form using the information about musical instruments. The field names have been given, but you must decide on the field types and lengths yourself.

When you have entered the data, print out the entire database. Then, select only those records for non-orchestral instruments and print them out. Search again for all records of non-orchestral instruments made of wood and print them out.

Field names
Category
Instrument
How played
Material
Use

Information to be entered in the database

```
TASK 76

INSTRUMENT          HOW PLAYED          MATERIAL          USE

STRING
Guitar              Strummed            Wood              Non-orchestral
Violin              Bowed               Wood              Orchestral
Cello               Bowed               Wood              Orchestral
Banjo               Strummed            Wood              Non-orchestral
Harp                Plucked             Wood              Both
Balalaika           Plucked             Wood              Non-orchestral

WIND
Flute               Air                 Silver            Orchestral
Bagpipes            Air                 Skin              Non-orchestral
Clarinet            Air                 Ebonite           Orchestral
Saxophone           Air                 Metal             Non-orchestral
Recorder            Air                 Wood              Non-orchestral

PERCUSSION
Kettledrums         Hammered            Copper            Orchestral
Cymbals             Struck              Brass             Orchestral
Xylophone           Hammered            Wood              Non-orchestral
```

Task 77

(1) Load your database program.

(2) Refer to the data given below and create an entry form containing the following fields, using abbreviations where necessary:

Field names
Department
Employee
Age
Job
Years service

(3) Enter the following details:

EMPLOYEE	AGE	JOB	SERVICE
FINANCE			
Buckley D	20	Accounts clerk	2
Barrington P	25	Book-keeper	3
Hughes M	36	Computer operator	8
Moore T	29	Word processor operator	7
MARKETING			
Callaghan H	30	Word processor operator	5
Eastgate D	44	Word processor operator	9
Baldwin P	29	Sales manager	10
Somerford R	41	Clerk	3
PERSONNEL			
Lennox A	33	Clerk	1
Upwood J	36	Word processor operator	6
Stanton W	27	Computer operator	2
Worthing B	19	Word processor operator	1

(4) Sort the records numerically in ascending order of age (i.e. youngest first).

(5) Print out the entire database.

(6) Delete the details for Baldwin who has now left the firm.

(7) Select those word processor operators who have more than 5 years service with the company.

(8) Print out the selected records.

■ Printing a partial database

Printing a partial database of selected fields

A partial database can be produced either by selecting only certain records for printing (which you have already been practising), or by selecting only certain fields for printing.

So far, you have always printed information from all the fields of your database, but very often all this information is not necessary. When this is the case, it is possible to choose exactly which fields you want to print.

FOOD	TYPE	COOKING METHOD	CALORIES PER 100 G
Beef	Meat	Roasting	365
Chicken	Poultry	Grilling	151
Duck	Poultry	Roasting	326
Venison	Game	Roasting	248
Salmon	Fish	Poaching	208

Database before selection

In this example, the information in the second field may not always be required, and if this is the case, the database can be printed without it.

FOOD	COOKING METHOD	CALORIES PER 100 G
Beef	Roasting	365
Chicken	Grilling	151
Duck	Roasting	326
Venison	Roasting	248
Salmon	Poaching	208

Partial database with only three fields printed

Printing a partial database of selected records and fields

It is also possible to make a selection of records first, and then print only selected fields for the chosen records.

For example, using the database given above, you may want to select only the details of roasted foods. Then, having made this selection, you may decide to print only the fields for FOOD and CALORIES PER 100 G. You would then be printing not only selected records, but selected fields for these records.

FOOD	CALORIES PER 100 G
Beef	365
Duck	326
Venison	248

Partial database with selected fields and records

Task 78

Design and create an entry form using the information about cinema shows. The field names have been given, but you must decide on the field types and lengths yourself.

When you have entered the data, print out the entire database. Then, select only the fields for CINEMA, FILM and TIMES and print them out.

Field names	Abbreviations
Cinema	NO = No of days showing
Film	Cont = Continuous
Category	Sep progs = Separate programmes
Times	
Late show	
No of days showing	

Information to be entered in the database

```
TASK 78

FILM                    CATEGORY      TIMES        LATE SHOW    NO


PLAZA
The Bid                 Thriller      Cont         11 pm         7
Once in a Lifetime      Romance       Sep progs    11.30 pm     21
Desert Riders           Western       Cont         None          3


RITZ
Hopping Mad             Cartoon       Cont         None         14
Once in a Lifetime      Romance       Sep progs    10.45 pm     21
Night Network           Thriller      Cont         11 pm         1
Golden Age              Comedy        Cont         11.15 pm      7


TIVOLI
The Bid                 Thriller      Cont         None          7
Dream Boat              Musical       Sep progs    None         28
Cut Your Cloth          Comedy        Cont         None          7
```

Task 79

Design and create an entry form using the information about local schools. The field names have been given, but you must decide on the field types and lengths yourself.

When you have entered the data, print out the entire database. Then, select only the records for primary schools and print them out. Finally, for these primary schools, select only the fields for SCHOOL, ROLL and INTAKE and print them out.

Field names
Area
School
Type
Roll
Intake
Uniform

Information to be entered in the database

TASK 79

SCHOOL	TYPE	ROLL	INTAKE	UNIFORM
ABINGTON				
St Michael's	Primary	250	Mixed	No
Parkside	Secondary	650	Mixed	Yes
Oakwood	Infant	150	Mixed	No
Abington Hall	Primary	200	Girls	Yes
Park West	Infant	150	Mixed	No
GREYTHORN				
Greythorn High	Secondary	550	Mixed	Yes
St Gregory's	Infant	150	Mixed	No
Linden Lea	Secondary	300	Boys	Yes
OVERTON				
The Vale	Primary	175	Boys	Yes
Princess Mary	Secondary	350	Girls	Yes
Overton Lane	Infant	100	Mixed	No
Manor House	Primary	220	Mixed	Yes

Task 80

Design and create an entry form using the information about equipment suppliers. The field names have been given, but you must decide on the field types and lengths yourself.

When you have entered the data, print out the entire database. Then, select only the records for suppliers in Manchester whose orders amount to more than £1000 and print them out. Finally, for these suppliers, select only the fields for SUPPLIER, EQUIPMENT and AMOUNT and print them out.

Field names
Date
Supplier
Town
Equipment
Order no
Amount £

Information to be entered in the database

```
TASK 80

SUPPLIER          TOWN          EQUIPMENT          ORDER NO    AMOUNT £

27 MARCH
Pricematch        Stockport     TVs                2143          925.50
Offtech Ltd       Widnes        School desks       2144         2500.00
Eurodesign        Manchester    Swivel chairs      2145         2300.50
Minerva Ltd       Runcorn       Wooden chairs      2146         1075.00
Greyscreen        Manchester    Computers          2147         3000.00

29 MARCH
PC Press          Liverpool     Printers           2148          500.50
Micro Systems     Manchester    Workstations       2149          950.00
VP View Ltd       Manchester    Videos             2150         1200.00

3 APRIL
PC Press          Liverpool     A4 paper           2151          150.00
Interprint        Manchester    Exercise books     2152         1100.00
Minerva Ltd       Runcorn       White boards       2153          350.50
Hi-tech           Manchester    Calculators        2154           85.50
```

Task 81

(1) Load your database program.

(2) Refer to the data given below and create an entry form for members of a badminton club containing the following fields, using abbreviations where necessary:

Field names
Gender
Name
Height
Weight
Age
Marital status

(3) Enter the following details:

NAME	HEIGHT	WEIGHT LB	AGE	STATUS
MALES				
Fitzgerald J	5ft 10in	135	29	Married
Dean S	6ft	144	34	Married
Weeks G	5ft 8in	128	23	Single
Newell D	5ft 9in	140	21	Single
Wilson M	5ft 6in	120	19	Single
Montague C	5ft 11in	155	30	Divorced
Donovan A	6ft	138	18	Single
FEMALES				
Scott M	5ft 5in	129	28	Divorced
Hodgkin S	5ft 2in	118	26	Single
Fletcher D	5ft 9in	142	23	Single
Stockport A	5ft 4in	124	31	Widowed
Boardwick J	5ft 3in	117	18	Single
Searle J	5ft 7in	128	24	Married
Ashmole C	5ft 6in	120	22	Married

(4) Sort the records alphabetically in ascending order (i.e. from A to Z).

(5) Erase the details for C. Montague and J. Searle who are no longer members of the badminton club. Add a record for a new female player as follows:

```
Hopson A     5ft 8in     138     20     Single
```

(6) Sort the records alphabetically in ascending order again.

(7) Save on disk and print out the entire database.

(8) Recall the file, make the corrections shown, and print out the entire database.

NAME	HEIGHT	WEIGHT LBS	AGE	STATUS
MALES				
Fitzgerald J	5ft 10in	135	29	Married
Dean S	6ft	144	34	*Single* ~~Married~~
Weeks G	5ft 8in	128	23	*Married* ~~Single~~
Newell D	5ft 9in	140	21	Single
Wilson M	5ft ~~6in~~ *8 in*	120	19	Single
~~Montague C~~	~~5ft 11in~~	~~155~~	~~30~~	~~Divorced~~
Donovan A	6ft	138	18	Single
FEMALES				
Scott M	5ft 5in	129	28	Divorced
Hodgkin S	5ft 2in	118	26	Single
Fletcher D	5ft ~~9in~~ *8 in*	142	23	Single
Stockport A	5ft 4in	*128* ~~124~~	31	Widowed
Boardwick J	5ft 3in	117	18	Single
~~Searle J~~	~~5ft 7in~~	~~128~~	~~24~~	~~Married~~
Ashmole C	5ft 6in	120	22	Married
Hopson A	*5ft 8in*	*138*	*20*	*Single*

(9) Select only those members who are 5ft 8in tall and print out the list.

(10) Select only those members who are single and who are aged under 30 years.

(11) Print out the list showing only **NAME**, **HEIGHT**, **WEIGHT** and **MARITAL STATUS**.

(12) Erase the file from disk and close down the system.

A prospectus is a printed document which gives details of the chief features of a school, college or business enterprise.

For Task 82, you must make a database which provides information about the courses run in your college or school. As with all databases, you must plan this out carefully on a piece of paper first, and then decide upon the field names, types and lengths.

The database may be very large if you include all the courses that your school or college offers, so it would be sensible to restrict it in some way. For example, you could include only the details of the sixth form courses offered, or, if you are at college, only the details of the business studies courses, or the sports courses.

List the field names that you are going to use. These could be things such as:

Field names
Course name
Course code
Level
Location
Fee

Below is a small example of the type of database you could design:

```
TASK 82


COURSE             CODE        LEVEL         LOCATION          FEE £


Keep Fit           S35         Beginners     Main Block         25
Yoga               H21         Advanced      Annexe             30
Badminton          S30         All           Main Block         25
Self Defence       H22         Beginners     Main Block         20
```

When you have entered the data, save on disk and print out the entire database.

Recall the database, sort it into ascending alphabetical order (from A to Z) and print it out again.

Then, make two different selections from your database and print them out. For example, select only the beginners courses and print them out, or select only the courses for advanced students which take place in the main block.

Make one further print-out of your own choosing – maybe you would like to add a new field to the database, such as a field describing the category of course (sports courses, in this example), or maybe you would like to change some of the details.

When you have completed the last print-out, erase the database from disk.